One Family's Response to Terrorism

This book honors the vision and dedicated service of

ARPENA SACHAKLIAN MESROBIAN,

director emerita (1975–1985) of Syracuse University Press,

who established the critically acclaimed series

Contemporary Issues in the Middle East.

*The portrait of Malcolm Kerr that now
hangs at the American University of Beirut.*

One Family's Response
to TERRORISM

A Daughter's Memoir

Susan Kerr van de Ven

Foreword by Saad Eddin Ibrahim

Syracuse University Press

First Paperback Edition 2010
10 11 12 13 14 15   6 5 4 3 2 1

The paper used in this publication meets the minimum requirements of American National Standard for Information Sciences—Permanence of Paper for Printed Library Materials, ANSI Z39.48-1984.∞™

For a listing of books published and distributed by Syracuse University Press, visit our Web site at SyracuseUniversityPress.syr.edu.

ISBN (paper): 978-0-8156-0954-4
ISBN (cloth): 978-0-8156-0873-8

Library of Congress Cataloging-in-Publication Data

The Library of Congress has cataloged the hardcover edition as follows:

Van de Ven, Susan Kerr.
   One family's response to terrorism : a daughter's memoir / Susan Kerr van de Ven ; foreword by Saad Eddin Ibrahim.
        p. cm. — (Contemporary issues in the Middle East)
   Includes bibliographical references and index.
   ISBN 978-0-8156-0873-8 (cloth : alk. paper)
  1. Kerr, Malcolm H.   2. Victims of terrorism—Lebanon—Biography.   3. Terrorism—Lebanon—Case studies.   4. American University of Beirut—Presidents—Biography.
5. College presidents—Lebanon—Beirut—Biography.   6. Van de Ven, Susan Kerr.
7. Americans—Middle East—Biography.   8. Arab-Israeli conflict.   9. Middle East—Politics and government—1945–   I. Title.
   HV6433.L4V36 2008
   363.325092—dc22
   [B]
   2007043871

For Ann and Hans

Susan Kerr van de Ven was born in 1958 at the American University Hospital in Beirut, Lebanon. She grew up mainly in California, but lived also in Egypt, Lebanon, France, England, and Tunisia. She was educated first at the American University in Cairo and Oberlin College, and then at Harvard University, where she received a master's degree in Middle Eastern studies and a doctorate in education.

She lives in Cambridge, England, with her husband and their three sons. She runs a creative writing program for children and serves as an elected Liberal Democrat councillor of Cambridgeshire County Council.

Her father, Malcolm Kerr, was assassinated on the campus of the American University of Beirut in 1984 while serving as the university's president.

Contents

Illustrations

Foreword

SAAD EDDIN IBRAHIM

THIS BOOK IS AN ODYSSEY of grief, a relentless search for truth, and finally a reconciliation. It starts for its author, Susan Kerr, with the nightmarish shock of the assassination of a loving father, leaving an aftermath of bewilderment and loss.

In her search for the truth surrounding her father's death, Susan ended up delving into an intertwined history of two countries, the United States and Lebanon, and its wider East-West context. Malcolm's death in 1984 presaged some of the celebrated and debated conundrums of Samuel Huntington's *Clash of Civilizations.* Like nested Russian dolls, the account narrated by Susan begins with her grandparents' tour of missionary duty in the Ottoman Empire following World War I. They were witness to the clashes between a besieged Armenian minority and zealous Young Turks trying to build a modern nation state out of a crumbling antique empire. The ensuing massacres claimed the lives of tens of thousands. This was a baptism for the Kerrs with Middle Eastern blood and fire. From that point onward in time and geography, three generations of the family would become eyewitnesses to a seemingly endless succession of tragic events spanning an entire century, four continents, another world war, regional revolutions, and civil and sectarian conflicts.

I happened to intersect with two generations of this exceptional family over the last forty-five years. Malcolm and I first met in 1963 at the University of California at Los Angeles (UCLA). He had just begun teaching as an assistant professor of political science, and I was a first year graduate student. When I was elected president of the campus chapter

of the Organization of Arab Students (OAS), I called on him as a potential faculty advisor. So youthful, almost boyish in looks and informally
dressed at our first encounter, I had to ask if he were Dr. Kerr or perhaps
the professor's student assistant. He must have encountered similar reactions from others because he smiled, pulled out his pack of cigarettes,
and lit one for each of us. He gave a quick sketch of his biography and
asked about mine. Malcolm was only six years older but without hesita-
tion he was our choice as OAS faculty advisor. During that first encounter he interspersed his conversation with many Lebanese Arabic words.
He put me at ease and quickly became a mentor and a friend.

A few months later, the OAS organized Palestine Week to raise awareness of the losses suffered during the 1948 war and partition. Meanwhile,
the Jewish students on campus were celebrating the fifteenth anniversary
of the establishment of the state of Israel. The two events were held too
close together, with passions too high on both sides, and the nearly inevitable happened—a violent clash broke out leading to several injuries
and much physical damage to the brand new student union building.
Campus security had to call in the Los Angeles Police for help in restor-
ing order. A campus and citywide uproar followed. Outnumbered and
with less popular support, the OAS and its faculty advisor were blamed
for what happened. Our organization was suspended, and I was advised
to transfer elsewhere. Young Malcolm's job, as well as his prospects for
tenure, were in jeopardy, yet he stood fast beside the OAS and demanded
an official investigation.

In an ironic twist, a local Jewish lawyer read news stories about the
incident and offered to defend us without cost. I hesitated in accepting
the offer until Malcolm encouraged me to do so. He was right, we got the
charges dropped, and I learned an early lesson in guarding against my
home-grown prejudices.

Malcolm and I parted ways shortly after, as I transferred to the University of Washington in Seattle to complete a Ph.D. Fifteen years later
we met again as faculty colleagues at the American University in Cairo
(AUC) and as neighbors in the suburb of Maadi. His wife, Ann, and my
wife, Barbara, soon became best friends. In the ensuing years, two of their

four children studied with me at AUC. My recollection is that Susan took every course I taught in those years. Malcolm would dryly warn her of the trouble I could get her in, from firsthand experience.

The Kerrs eventually returned to UCLA, and I was invited by Malcolm to join a team undertaking research on the emerging new Arab sociopolitical order that resulted from the oil boom of the 1970s. A volume edited by Malcolm, *Rich and Poor States in the Middle East,* as well as an authored book of my own, *The New Arab Social Order,* came out of this collaboration. The early friendship was by now being cemented by family ties and academic cooperation. Susan babysat for our two children both in Cairo and in Los Angeles. Steve Kerr, a rising basketball star, was a hero for our children. We shared everyone's joy when Malcolm attained a lifelong dream and was appointed president of the American University of Beirut.

Reading Susan's manuscript these many years later, I could still feel her anguish and recall our own pain on learning that Malcolm had been shot and killed outside his campus office in Beirut. But it is her maturity in incorporating that tragedy into her life and grappling with it that struck me this time. In remembering her as a playful student, I failed to take note of her maturation over the thirty years since leaving my classroom. She had gone on to Harvard for a graduate degree and had done service learning tours among Palestinian children, teaching English and art at St. George's School in Jerusalem. In short, Susan had been polished as a bonafide scholar and sensitized as a social activist. All of these accumulated life experiences were called upon to help her live through and make sense of her father's assassination.

Her excavation of the many layers of Middle Eastern politics in this fine book is matched by an exploration of her own soul as well as the imagined world of her father's killer. There is no patronizing or justification made for the ugly deed of violence, only a relentless pursuit of understanding. This is a perspective on war and hatred brought home forcefully by an intensely personal narrative.

And in the end, because there can never be complete unraveling of the impulse to kill, it is also a testament to the individuals who try instead to bridge gaping cultural divides. The greatest homage that could be paid to a scholar and bridge-builder like Malcolm Kerr is to have left among his many legacies a remarkable daughter to tell his story.

Cairo

June 2007

Acknowledgments

THIS BOOK IS A PERSONAL ACCOUNT of a judgment of evidence concerning my father's assassination in Lebanon in 1984. I have had much help in trying to learn and explore, but the conclusions drawn are my own.

The material presented here is the product not of a historian, but of a plaintiff in a lawsuit, seeking to understand as broadly as possible the facts surrounding a particular case. I have had the benefit of access to documents gathered under a Freedom of Information Act search, and a wealth of personal papers once belonging to my father but now in my possession. I have had, too, the privilege of access to extraordinary people with extraordinary knowledge of historical events in Lebanon.

Although a trial has taken place, and research in preparation for this book has been conducted, an open mind concerning the complex history of 1980s Lebanon is something I hope always to keep.

As a graduate student at Harvard, a seminar on Peace and Conflict Resolution with Professor Herb Kelman laid a foundation stone for this project—though at the time I didn't know that I would one day need in a personal way the principles being disseminated by my teacher.

I have had the opportunity to speak with a number of Lebanese, Palestinian, Egyptian, Israeli, British, and American acquaintances about their experiences of political violence, and this has helped me to understand my own.

Among the many friends who have provided useful insights and comments on the manuscript are Yahya Sadowski, Fawaz Gerges, Gail Gerhart, Necla Tschirgi, Reginald Bartholomew, Paul Jabber, Ben Weir, John Waterbury, Dorothy Thompson, Marion Clarkstone, Jackie Somani, and my father's sister, Dorothy Kerr Jessup. Michael Martinez and Stuart New-berger helped me to sift through and understand legal documents relating to our case. Barbara Ras and Naomi Shihab Nye helped me to get started on the project of writing, and Mary Selden Evans and John Fruehwirth at Syracuse University Press encouraged me to see the book through.

Special thanks to Hala Es-Said Cochrane and Chana Arnon for per-mission to quote from personal correspondence, and to Yasma Fuleihan for permission to reprint a photograph of her husband, Basil, from the Ameri-can University of Beirut 1984 student yearbook. David Dodge has been a gracious friend and point of reference from the inception of this project.

I am grateful to Saad Eddin Ibrahim, my professor at the American University in Cairo who taught the example of activism, for writing the foreword.

Revisiting a painful past is not something to be done alone. My three brothers, Andrew, John, and Steve, have given me their own special mix-ture of support—whether dissecting information, thrashing out a moral dilemma, or reminding me of the unbreakable bond that holds us to-gether. My three sons, Johan, Derek, and Willem, at much younger ages than their uncles, have given me the very same—plus the day-to-day joy of living under the same roof. My mother, Ann, and my husband, Hans, have been my partners through thick and thin, both with the gift of living life to the fullest.

One Family's Response to Terrorism

Prologue

BACK IN THE GOOD OLD DAYS, when terrorism was still at a nuisance level, my father used to supplement the family income by writing disaster scenarios for Middle East watchers in the U.S. government.

The task would be to write a series of four or five scenarios in order to create a sense of possibility. One scenario might predict the assassination of some long-standing political leader that would throw the whole balance of power in the region into disarray. Two or three others might predict new Arab-Israeli wars erupting on various borders. Such wars might be what Dad called the "garden variety," or they might be big ones with catastrophic consequences. A final scenario might rest upon some subtle alteration to a complicated geopolitical alliance with wide-ranging, dangerous implications. Dad might call this one the "Humpty Dumpty scenario." I would be dumbstruck at the range of possible disasters and think my father the cleverest man in the world for thinking of them all.

Dad also testified in court cases involving plane crashes. He was the expert witness, explaining the ins and outs behind the blowing up of some plane originating from or bound for a Middle Eastern destination. One of those cases, I remember quite clearly, earned him a whole $2,000. "And I only have to travel Back East twice for this!" he'd exclaimed. Such an influx of cash might not get us out of the red, but it would be a welcome addition in a large household trying to get by on an academic salary.

Not all of Dad's extra jobs were so outlandish. He hated being on the University of California budget committee, but that earned a solid $6,000 per year, which in the early 1970s was a figure not to be sneezed at.

Royalties from his books—one of which was a classic in the field—were always a delightful extra. Dad would rush into the kitchen waving the yellow printed sheet in the air and announce, "Hey everyone, *The Arab Cold War* made $32 last month. Let's go to Paris for the weekend!"

One can't help wondering how a man who was forever struggling to keep the family budget out of the red could have been deemed an asset to something as important as the university budget committee. I guess I'll never know the answer to that question.

Similarly, it is ironic that a man noted for his Middle Eastern disaster scenarios, and one who had the gift of native understanding of the region, did not describe the very scenario that would dictate his own death: that of the policy of violent elimination of Westerners from Lebanese soil in the 1980s.

When it happened that Dad was shot and killed outside his office door at the American University of Beirut, just eighteen months into his dream (and higher-paying) job as AUB's president, a crushing range of possible explanations for his assassination came into view—a very messy set of scenarios indeed. Was it the Lebanese Christians, who were mad at Dad for his sympathetic stance toward the country's Muslims? Was it the Israelis, who were mad at Dad for throwing their roaming, insensitive soldiers out of the campus gates (scolding them, as he did so, in fluent Arabic)? Was it, one wondered half-jokingly, the CIA? Or was it, as the anonymous caller to the Agence France-Presse claimed, the Islamic Jihad (whoever they were)?

Indeed, anything was possible in January of 1984. Lebanon had been in the throes of a civil war for eight years, and layered upon that cycle of domestic violence were other wars being fought by outsiders: the Israelis, whose army had occupied the south of Lebanon and pounced on Beirut in the summer of 1982; the Americans, whose warships had famously fired shells the size of Volkswagens into the mountains behind Beirut (and then suffered, perhaps in retaliation, the bombing of their embassy and marine barracks); the Syrians, with their long-standing offer to take over the tiny but strategically placed country; and more recently the Iranians, whose Revolutionary Guard had set up headquarters in the ancient city of Baalbek and were working in tandem with local friends and relations to bring the Islamic revolution to Lebanon.

Even while rumors flew as to the identity of the culprits in the matter of the assassination of Malcolm Kerr, many of the suspects themselves paid tribute to Dad. In a rare show of unity, the warring factions marked his death with an official period of mourning across Beirut. They attended his memorial service, like us paying no heed to anonymous threats to blow up the chapel where the service was to be held. In the condolence line afterward, my brand-new and stunned husband, now the eldest male in the family, was confided in by one factional leader, who assured him, "We didn't do it!"

We never got very far with the question of who'd killed Dad and why. Then and in the years that followed, any pursuit of the matter quickly dried up. For given the anarchic state of affairs in Lebanon, how could any orderly investigation stand a chance of success? "You will never know" was the advice given more than once. The university itself never even bothered to request the police report of January 18, 1984—a reflection of the mood of resignation, of the irrelevance of the police in wartime, or perhaps from a desire to ruffle no feathers in a deadly atmosphere. The U.S. government, as far as we could tell, had no idea who'd killed Dad and made no official response to the assassination of the second highest-ranking American in Beirut, apart from a public condemnation of the act and condolences to us.

In any case we, Dad's family, were consumed with grief and had no resources for anything but taking one day at a time. Each of us had been thrust into a new world in which one person was no longer present: someone who'd been loved and cherished and who had figured in all visions of the future.

The range of our individual experiences of grief in the aftermath of Dad's death was as bewildering as the range of possible explanations for his death. Nineteen years passed before we were able to come together as a family and respond collectively to the disaster that had befallen us.

By this time, the phenomenon of terrorism was no longer just our problem. Indeed I heard U.S. Assistant Defense Secretary Paul Wolfowitz say so in a BBC interview one evening in November 2001. In the wake of September 11, he announced, terrorism was no longer the nuisance it had once been. I wanted to scream at him. How could anyone characterize

Andrew, John, and Ann receiving condolences at AUB, January 20, 1984.

terrorism in such terms? My heart sank as I realized that Mr. Wolfowitz had, in a moment, stoked the very fires of anti-Americanism.

How to respond to terrorism became the foremost question on everyone's mind, not just in America but also around the world. While some seemed to find instant answers, our own still tentative stance was the result of nearly two decades of soul-searching and the delicate building of family consensus. But whatever doubts we had, we did know that if our grievance was about violence, then our response to it must bear none of its hallmarks. If our concern was about the degradation of human life, our response must be nothing but humane.

This book is about what happened to us as a family in the wake of one death by terrorism, and the moral choices we felt compelled to take, at long last, toward legal justice. It is about understanding the truth, and holding governments to account for their policies and actions.

In the end, Dad himself through his writings helped me to understand the broad forces that had contributed to the problem of anti-Western terrorism in Lebanon in the 1980s and, sadly, its metamorphosis into the problem of terrorism as we know it today. I never anticipated that the painstaking process of information gathering would transform into an embrace of knowledge, which in turn would dispel at last my sense of panic and fear of the unknown. Knowledge has isolated the problem rather than enlarged it, and somehow, through the delineation of fact and fiction, offered a sense of hope for the future.

1

Breaking Apart

THE NEWSPAPER PHOTOGRAPH of the space shuttle *Columbia* breaking up and splintering down through the clear blue sky above Texas struck me at once as a matching image of our family's splintering after Dad's assassination. I pictured the astronauts, still alive but trapped in separate burning compartments of the broken shuttle as it plummeted down toward Earth. They died together, and yet each one was alone. That was what happened to us, except that the process was slower . . . and rebirth was possible.

Another image that absorbed my mind some dozen years after Dad's death, when signs of rebirth were at long last evident to me, was that of the bullet that had entered the back of his head on that Wednesday morning. I imagined its path, first ruining his fantastic brain and then exiting his forehead and shattering the horn-rimmed frames of his glasses. I saw it ricochet against the walls of College Hall, striking my mother as she came running up the stairs to find out what had happened to her husband. It bounced hard off her and onto my youngest and angriest brother, Andrew, as he listened to the radio news of his father's death at a school café several blocks away. The bullet was alive, it seemed, and had an endless, menacing capacity to move and inflict damage. It struck my brother John when he arrived from Cairo the next day and left a permanent mark on his expression. It ricocheted and knocked me senseless when I picked up the telephone at my honeymoon home in Taiwan and heard my mother's gentle voice telling me there was bad news. It struck my brother Steve with such force as to push him wildly onto the streets of Tucson, Arizona, where he could not stop running in the aftermath

6

of his middle-of-the-night phone call. The sound of howling rose from everywhere and the bullet continued to fly, touching and wounding everyone in its path.

The ricochet effect of Dad's death, as I saw it, meant that every relationship connected to him was affected. His removal from the core of the family left wires loose and dangling so that we no longer functioned properly, whether as a group or as individuals. For me, the establishment of a new married life took on totally new and absurd challenges. For Steve and John, fleeing the nest at eighteen or twenty-one involved previously unimagined dimensions. For Andrew, the normal vicissitudes of the teenage years were superseded by unnatural ones. The black hole of my mother's widowhood, not to mention its appearance at the tender age of forty-nine, was incomprehensible to my brothers and me, who were too inexperienced to understand the implications of the sudden loss of one's primary relationship and point of reference. Outside the family, too, relationships changed; some friendships were strengthened, but others fell by the wayside. Somehow, it was necessary to disengage from the tangled mess and begin anew as individuals. Only then could the process of rewiring a family structure begin. But all that came many years later.

The details of the breaking apart of the individual and the family that accompanies bereavement are intimate and difficult to share. They are frightening to discuss with loved ones and make no sense to talk about with strangers. The effect is the compounding of one's newfound isolation.

And yet, to argue for a nonviolent response to terrorism, one must establish for the public record the intimate way in which violence destroys the fabric of human life. It is necessary to lay down the facts in order to show that any response that adds to the spectrum of human wreckage makes no sense, even though for some it might seem impossible to resist the urge to strike back.

Many Jews tell us that we must never forget the Holocaust; we must never visit that site of inhumanity again. One way in which this message is conveyed is by displaying pictures of the Holocaust in its full obscenity so that, even if we know that human beings were gassed to death or shot naked into their own graves, the vision of raw photographic detail can bring us to a dramatically higher level of comprehension. Chinese historians do the same in their Museum of the Nanjing Massacre, showing frame by frame the beheading of a local resident by a Japanese officer. By looking at these seemingly impossible human images we are reminded of what happens in war and we are urged as human beings to conquer our awful weaknesses. In Britain, bereavement was at one time so widespread that the heart of the tiniest village bears a memorial to its youthful inhabitants lost in the two world wars. Where violence has taken human life, memorials are instinctively erected both as tribute but also as a plea against its recurrence. Even accidental traffic deaths result in spontaneous roadside markers showing where someone has been killed and urging drivers to take care and slow down. It is a relentless but essential task to remind ourselves of past mistakes.

In the case of wrongful death, the court requires for the public record a statement as to the effects of that death on the plaintiff. For the plaintiff, this statement might prove a powerful affirmation of the injustice one has experienced. Equally, it might be humiliating to have to state publicly what seems so obvious. Or, one might suffer indignity at having to reveal what feels intimate. But like the war memorial or the roadside altar, a public statement about bereavement is required as a sort of foundation in the process of putting things right.

This requirement, with its range of accompanying emotions, was made of our family when we brought forward a lawsuit against the government of Iran for its sponsored killing of Dad. Although our presence in the U.S. District Court reflected our having come together as a family, our individual testimonies emphasized the uniqueness of our individual perspectives and journeys.

My own breaking apart took place within the parallel needs of building of a new marriage and wanting to be with my grieving mother and bereft younger brothers—though this was physically impossible, because we were separated by continents. Nevertheless, an emotional tug-of-war began inside me. When I was not preoccupied with family relationships, there was the opportunity to be sucked down by a solitary sense of despair. As if mimicking my emotions, my body stopped working properly. One by one my joints stiffened up until I could hardly move. I was

With Dad on the eve of my wedding, July 1983. It was the last time I would see him.

introduced to the rheumatologist who would befriend me and issued a wheelchair by the Harvard Infirmary, which I held onto for the next few years. The sense of isolation intensified.

One afternoon I knocked an inflamed elbow against the wall. I remember being absolutely overcome with pain, and because I was alone I let myself succumb to sobbing. Once I started, there was no turning back. It came in waves, and after a while I discovered that behind the first layer, another confronted me, for after I had finally finished crying through the physical pain I came, as if in a nightmare, to another door through which I had to pass—a door leading into that thick, dense jungle of grief. The expression "to shed" tears is certainly apt, for there comes with sobbing a vivid sensation of trying to rid oneself of some kind of poison. I was stunned when finally the sobbing came to an end, but I was also aware that a vast amount of poison was still inside me.

It is impossible to know the inner turmoil of another, though evidence of the breaking apart of other members of my family was evident from the outside. Andrew lost much of the memory of our father. At night he wore a mouth guard to prevent the grinding down of his teeth. Years later, while testifying for that essential public record, he described the torture of listening to the sobs of our mother. At first he would try to comfort her. But after a couple of years he could stand her sobbing no longer and would shut himself in his room. He kept away from the awful sound but hated knowing that he was unable to help someone in his family who was suffering nearby.

Anna Blundy, whose journalist father, David Blundy, was shot and killed in El Salvador, describes in her book *Every Time We Say Goodbye* the splintering of her emotional being in the aftermath of her father's death.[1] Like me, she lived what was by any standards a privileged life in terms of education and the support of family and friends. And yet beneath the veneer of her Oxford degree and her budding newspaper career was an abyss into which she fell and in which she slipped around for years, until somehow she received a signal that life can still go on. She realized that it was in her power to make it happen if she began to climb out of the hole she was in.

As for me, I robotically completed my doctorate, which was at least a symbol of progress, and celebrated wedding anniversaries with my husband. Illness slowly abated but left infertility in its wake, until many years later when—by some miracle—we had children. They, of course, were the first true signs of rebirth.

While all this private breaking apart took place, a heroic image of Dad and the portrayal of his surviving family as wholesome and persevering were publicly perpetuated. It was true that Dad had been courageous, but the thirst for a tragic story was disconcerting. *Reader's Digest* and *People* magazine regurgitated the tale. Steve's growing fame in the world of college and professional basketball widened the audience, and countless sportswriters around the country kept the outlines of the family story in print. A Hollywood screenplay was written and novelists were inspired. Most of it was not distasteful, except for the occasional rendition that would upset one of us. One novelist in the mid-1990s spun the tale of a widowed mother and daughter in a blend of academia and the developing world, with events spinning out of control until the daughter's husband is violently killed somewhere in South America. The daughter, like me a mother of twin boys, is left widowed like her mother before her.

Henry Bromell's *Little America* was published seventeen years after Dad's death and reviewed in the *New York Times*.[2] It drew openly on the bare outlines of the Malcolm Kerr story; even the name of the principal character, Mack Hooper, was taken from Dad's childhood nickname and middle name. In a nauseating twist, Mack Hooper was a CIA man rather than an academic, planting the suggestion that the real Malcolm Kerr had been somehow part of that murky world of deception—the very world outside of which Dad had stood and that yet had claimed his life like a pawn in a political chess game.

Myth making grew and perpetuated the tragic and glamorous elements of the story. These retellings always focused on personalities and rarely taught anything about the broader circumstances and suffering of that wider community in Lebanon or the Middle East generally that were surely linked to Dad's death and indeed to the growing problem of terrorism. That we lacked information as to the question of exactly who had killed Dad was in this context almost unimportant. What was worrying was the confinement of the scope of interest. Our story became akin to a soft TV drama, as opposed to an inducement for an in-depth investigative news program.

.   .   .

Another concern for me, also difficult to express, was about the uncountable, inevitable breakings apart of bereaved individuals and families in the wake of other acts of violence in Lebanon.

As soon as Dad's memorial service was over, my family said good-bye to Lebanon. That was not an easy thing to do, given that Lebanon had been, off and on, home to our extended family for over sixty years. Seven Kerrs had been born there between 1925 and 1965 and the next generation would have been entitled to Lebanese citizenship—something I always wished for as a child. Still, when life there was no longer possible, there were other places to go. My mother was offered a job at the American University in Cairo, where she and Dad had taught before, and she took Andrew there to live. A brass plaque on the door of their new apartment read, in Arabic and English, "The A. Kerrs." They stayed for five years, John joining them for the first two, and nursed their internal injuries with the help of a large collection of old friends who understood something of what had happened because they had known Dad and were, like him, of the place.

But our loss was an exception to the rule, for we were able to leave war behind and go just about anywhere we wanted. The image of our unseen counterparts haunted me from the beginning and I wondered constantly what was happening to them.

The sounds of Lebanon were native to me: the braying of donkeys on a mountain path; the call to prayer that inevitably made me stop everything I was doing so as to give myself over to its wonderful, imploring music; the honking of taxi horns, which I somehow also loved; the terrifying noise of gunfire close by, always accompanied by visions of flame jutting from the gun's barrel; and the distinctive high-pitched wailing of women, produced by a rapid clicking movement of the tongue, which signified joy—or death.

I could not help thinking about Lebanese families who, like mine, had been maimed by violence. When I did, a picture of the whole of Lebanon ablaze would inevitably rise up. For I knew that death was rampant, and that the death of a Lebanese and its accompanying implications stood a good chance of being unfathomably worse than that which we had experienced. Some might argue that death is death and violence is violence, but to discount differences of circumstance would, I felt, mean blindness to a growing crisis: the crisis of the young person bereft of any hope or opportunity.

.   .   .

A BBC *Panorama* documentary that investigated the criminal responsibility of Ariel Sharon in the massacre of many hundreds of Palestinians in the Sabra and Shatila refugee camps of Beirut in September 1982 contained interviews with a handful of survivors, all of whom had witnessed the executions of loved ones. I could only marvel at their ability to stand up and speak at all. For apart from the trauma of those hellish few days, these people had been born in refugee camps and were by definition part of an unbroken cycle of homelessness that spanned generations. Their families had been forced to leave their homes in Palestine and then had moved from camp to camp—from Israel to the West Bank in 1948, on to Jordan in 1967, and then to Lebanon a few years later. Wherever they were forced to go, they were considered a liability.

As the Palestinian refugees migrated to new camps in new countries, Lebanon's burgeoning Shi'ite population sank into its own homelessness and poverty. There were many reasons for this sinking; one was the fighting between newly arrived Palestinians and neighboring Israelis in traditionally Shi'ite South Lebanon. Lebanese Shi'ites were literally caught in the crossfire: those whose homes were bulldozed by a vengeful Israeli army made their way as refugees to Beirut. Traditionally excluded from education and social welfare, these Shi'ites had little to offer, and ironically some found shelter in the Palestinian camps of South Beirut. Reports claimed that a large proportion of those massacred at Sabra and Shatila were in fact Shi'ite refugees.

The overlapping misfortunes of Lebanon's Palestinians and Shi'ites are key to understanding the evolution of the organized, violent, anti-Western campaign that reached the front pages of the Western press in the 1980s. The overwhelming forces that come down on an individual and cause him or her to break apart in the wake of violent loss cannot but be horribly compounded in such dire circumstances as these Lebanese Shi'ites and Palestinians endured.

Robert Baer's book *See No Evil* is the memoir of a CIA case officer's life spent largely in the Middle East and for three years in mid-1980s in Lebanon.[3] It is an account of an obsessive quest for the culprits in the bombing of the U.S. Embassy in Beirut in April 1983. Baer's own people were in that building: the CIA's Beirut staff was literally decimated and, in Baer's view, left an American intelligence vacuum that would prove difficult to fill. In Baer's personal quest to piece together the story behind this hugely important suicide bombing, he builds composite sketches of the individuals in his pool of suspects.

One of these is Imad Mughniyeh. Perhaps an extreme example of my unseen counterpart, Mughniyeh was, like me, born in Lebanon in the late 1950s/early 1960s. He was raised in Beirut and we might have passed each other near the airport along whose runway he grew up. Planes I flew in came within a few hundred feet of the corrugated tin rooftop of his shanty home.

Both of us were drawn to work in a Palestinian community in our first flush of independence. I went to teach at St. George's School in Arab East Jerusalem, and he joined Yasser Arafat's elite bodyguard in Beirut. I was paid a pittance to teach art and English to five hundred Arabic-speaking boys, and he was given the lowly job of sniper on Beirut's Green Line at the heart of the Lebanese civil war. Baer says that Mughniyeh, a Shi'ite, received no formal Islamic education. While he sniped and dodged bullets, I, of Presbyterian stock, moved on to graduate school and studied Islamic history.

In 1982, the year I met my husband, Mughniyeh met Ali Akbar Mohtashemi, the Iranian ambassador to Syria. Mohtashemi's real commission was Lebanon, where he came with money, highly trained soldiers, a sophisticated intelligence infrastructure, and a vision for implementing the Islamic revolution. I traveled to Beirut that year to see Dad inaugurated as AUB's new president, and my plane flew over Mughniyeh's family home once again. By this time Mughniyeh was probably already aware of a general interest in assassinating my father, though he personally was immersed in plans to blow up the U.S. Embassy—a target higher on the list. I don't know how many of Mughniyeh's extended family had been killed so far in the endless civil war, or how. Shot at close range? Crushed in a bombed building? Set ablaze? I don't know whether he was driven by anger or ideology or even insanity, but certainly society all around him had long been crumbling, and while in my terms there was little hope or opportunity for young people, still a person could do literally whatever he wanted.

A year or so later both targets on the list had been hit, and I joined the crowded way station of people breaking apart.

2

First Reactions

FOR THE NEXT SEVERAL YEARS, wearing the mouth guard at night and losing the memory of his father, Andrew dreamed about the pleasure of killing Dad's assassins.

After hearing the news on the radio at the school café, he had taken off and run all over the AUB campus, looking for our mother. The campus guards wouldn't let him through the gate across from the hospital, so he climbed over it. Still he couldn't find her. He ran back again through the campus and finally they met at Marquand House, the official residence of the university president. His first words, shouted, were, "I want to get those guys!"

He was alone, for no one in the family shared that desire. There was no one with whom to sound off those vengeful thoughts, and dreams became his way of doing so—though we didn't know about that torment until years later. I remember my ordinary teenage torments, of boys and diets and mood swings, and don't like to think about Andrew's. He moved to Egypt and passed the days going to school at Cairo American College. His friends there were to become the most important of his life because they'd known Dad and understood the essence of what had happened to him, and Andrew didn't have to explain anything.

Not only did no one in the family share Andrew's vengeful desires, but no one in any official capacity took any initiative to find the killers and bring them to justice. The contents of the Lebanese police report were never divulged to us and never requested by AUB. The university was peopled by men and women trying simply to survive until the next day, and pursuing a police investigation was somehow not on the agenda.

In any case, Dad's murder was no isolated event. AUB's acting president, David Dodge, had been kidnapped a few weeks before Dad arrived in Beirut in the summer of 1982, and a spate of killings and kidnappings marked the rest of the decade. Besides the soon-to-be famous names of its kidnapped Western faculty members, who included Peter Kilburn, the university librarian; Joseph Cicippio, the university accountant; David Jacobsen, the hospital director; Tom Sutherland, the dean of agriculture; and Brian Keenan and many other members of the English Department, AUB lost scores of Lebanese whose names never made the headlines of the Western press.

Haj Omar was a university driver who had a reputation for making things happen when most people were too scared to journey to some essential destination. He would venture out during the 1982 Israeli aerial bombardment of Beirut, in search of emergency fuel for the university hospital. He once drove Steve and two other faculty boys over the dangerous road to Damascus during the shelling of Beirut's airport, so that they could get back to their respective schools in America and England on time. I knew Haj Omar because he'd met my plane three days after Dad's death when my mother had been advised to avoid a public meeting. He'd also met my plane when John and I had flown to Beirut a year before to surprise Dad at his inauguration ceremony. When I saw him this time I broke down and literally cried on his shoulder. I can still see his kind, tired, and flinching face as he waited for me to compose myself. A few years later Haj Omar was shot and killed by a sniper while driving across town. His murder symbolized the gradual disabling of the university and the random nature of violence as so many people knew it.

There were other perhaps sinister forces behind AUB's failure to pursue officially the assassination of its president—in his own office, no less, in the heart of the campus and in the university's hallmark building, College Hall. Indeed, this murder had pointed to the absolute vulnerability of the place. The point was underscored eight years later when a huge bomb was detonated in College Hall itself, bringing it down and weakening the foundations of other key university buildings nearby. And yet nothing at all was done in response. A new president was hired and a new building was erected. Life went on, but justice could not be pursued in a lawless society. Anarchy meant that killers were everywhere, and to provoke them would be suicidal.

The U.S. government, too, left the matter alone, even though it cited Dad's death as one in a string of attacks on American institutions in Lebanon that would not be tolerated. What was that supposed to mean?

Traditional justice did not figure in the complex game of international diplomacy, when the mutual interests of opposing sides might collide for a brief time, resulting in the oddest of agreements. The arms-for-hostages deal, also known as the Iran-Contra Affair, was the most stunning publicly exposed example of unorthodox diplomacy of those crisis years. It took place in 1986, when members of the Reagan administration assisted in the illegal sale of arms to Iran, and then used the proceeds to help fund, also illegally, the Nicaraguan Contra organization, which used terror tactics in working to undermine the Nicaraguan government.

Whatever intelligence the U.S. government acquired in the case of Dad's assassination went not to us, nor to his employer, nor even to the Lebanese police, but to a host of U.S. government agencies in whose jurisdiction the information was deemed relevant. It was classified, and even now the most essential pieces are inaccessible to anyone from the outside. Thus in addition to the absence of justice, there was for years a total blackout on information. If one wanted fair and proper recourse, it simply wasn't in the realm of possibility.

Contrary to Andrew's instincts, I felt no compelling need to find Dad's killers and bring them to justice. To me this contrast illustrated as much as anything the innate differences between human beings. Andrew and I were as close as siblings could be. He was born when I was nearly ten, and we were almost inseparable in the years I helped to raise him. Yet our basic reactions to the murder of our father were in some ways polar opposites. Mine was a desperate need to understand and forgive.

My mother shared my reactions and has pointed out to me that these feelings are at once moral and practical. They reflected for both of us an instinct for survival. She believes that hatred eats away at people, and she warned Andrew against succumbing to it—knowing all the while that we cannot necessarily change inborn ways of feeling and thinking.

From the day of Dad's memorial service in the AUB chapel, my mother endeavored to understand and to help others to do so. She bravely stood up before the congregation and delivered a tribute to Dad, setting out all the good reasons why together they had decided to come to Beirut and to work for AUB. Their belief in building bridges across cultures, through institutions of education, was a thread running through her book, *Come with Me from Lebanon,* the writing of which took many years and was both cathartic and painful.[1] Over the years following its publication, it was evident that her aim of imparting understanding, rather than blame, had reached many people.

For me, understanding and forgiveness reflected in part an impulse to move away from the human capacity for evil and violence that had just visited itself upon my family. I had no interest in prolonging my acquaintance with the bearer of the gun. When I did imagine the killer, I conjured up a dreamlike vision of human form, and always it came out from under the exploding shells of the USS *New Jersey* as it fired away onto the shores of Lebanon. The shape belonged to a young person who had been the recipient not just of bad luck but of the fallout of relentless, dirty, and deadly political game playing—and now we had something in common. We had been thrust, in different clothing, into the same lifeboat. I felt an actual bond of some sort with the imagined killer, since I could empathize with his (I assumed) feelings of rage.

If those were my instincts, and even if they were in some ways naïve, they were fed by a reservoir of humanitarian tradition exemplified over many years by my grandparents and passed down to the next generation. Stanley and Elsa Kerr belonged to that breed of American humanist "missionary" of the early twentieth century who, at a time when travel and communication were arduous and uncertain, left everything familiar behind and went to an unknown land of people in need.

My grandparents met on the road to Marash, southern Turkey, in 1921. Elsa, who had a degree from Beloit College in Wisconsin, had completed a year of Turkish language study in Constantinople and was on her way to begin teaching math at Marash Girls' College. For a woman of her day, her education, independence, and idealism were breathtaking.

Stanley Kerr (right, in uniform) with Armenian refugees preparing Armenian Christmas dinner in Marash, Turkey, January 19, 1920.

Stanley had traveled to Turkey to work under the auspices of the American Committee for Near East Relief. Energetic and adventurous, he had already spent a year in Marash in 1919–20 when he witnessed the siege of the town by Turkish Nationalists in which half of the town's Armenian population was brutally killed. The town's French garrison, intended to provide order and protection under the agreements of the Paris Peace Conference, had withdrawn in anticipation of Turkish attack, leaving the vulnerable Armenians exposed. The task of the Near East Relief in 1921 was the essential care of Marash's Armenian survivors, now refugees, and soon, their final evacuation from the town as Turkish Nationalist aims were realized. A witness to unfolding history, Stanley recorded these events in a memoir, *The Lions of Marash*.[2]

What happened in Marash said much about the post–World War I landscape of the Eastern Mediterranean and North Africa, when Allied powers had divided up the administration of the defeated Ottoman

Empire and its sprawling domain. Domestic political games and animosi-
ties met with the clumsy and inconsistent enforcement of the Allied administration. The Turkish Nationalist movement's pursuit of an independent
Turkish state depended, in its terms, on the elimination of the established
Armenian population, whether by expulsion or by organized slaughter,
and also of course on the removal of the Allied military presence. The
deadly pursuit of these aims at Marash hinted at the broad evolving political picture of the time. Early nationalism was emerging on a map recently
redrawn by Western powers whose understanding of the region and ability to carry out its own stated aims were tenuous.

Stanley and Elsa found the basis for a life's work in these circumstances.
Like other Americans of their time, they openly expressed criticism and
concern over the responsibilities and actions of their own government in
a region that they sought personally to serve. They assisted in the evacuation of the Armenian refugees from Marash and then continued their mission by running an orphanage for Armenian children near Byblos, north
of Beirut, in what was at that time called Greater Syria. By 1925 Stanley
had acquired a Ph.D. in biochemistry and was appointed by President Ba-
yard Dodge to the faculty of the American University of Beirut—founded
by American missionaries in 1866 and by now formally established as
a secular liberal arts institution. Elsa taught math and social work at a
nearby junior college and later became the advisor to women students at
AUB. Ties with the local Armenian community endured, and friendships
with Lebanese colleagues developed. In that setting they raised their four
children and lived out their working lives.

While the benevolent American tradition of human service was taking root in the Middle East, Western politicians continued to grapple with
domestic problems and politics of the region. And so, various Western
concerns became involved both in contributing to, and trying to resolve,
problems in a land far from home.

To the south of Turkey and Greater Syria lay Palestine, a mostly rural
territory but one with a strong religious and intellectual center in Jerusalem. Its Arabic-speaking population comprised chiefly Sunni Muslims
but also Christians and Jews. The late nineteenth century saw the origins
of the Zionist movement, in which European Jews established colonies, or

settlements, in Palestine. The movement gained official sanction through the blessing of Britain in 1917 in what became known as the Balfour Declaration, when Secretary of State for Foreign Affairs Lord Balfour wrote to a prominent British Jew, Baron Lionel Walter de Rothschild, promising support for a Zionist national home in Palestine.

With the end of World War I a year later and the redrawing of the Middle Eastern map by the war's Allied victors, Britain took on the administration of Palestine as a mandate, which facilitated the realization of the Balfour Declaration. Zionist colonization of Palestine increased, as did local Arab concern at the changing demographic makeup of their native land. Hitler's Holocaust spurred on the Jewish settlement of Palestine, and Arab concern intensified. Clashes between the local Arabs and Jewish settlers became more frequent, and Britain's hold on its protectorate began to slip, until finally Britain decided to withdraw altogether in 1947, leaving those Arab-Jewish clashes to erupt into outright war. That war became known in Arabic as *al-nakba,* or "the catastrophe."

In 1948 the State of Israel was declared, and the first generation of Palestinian refugees was created. The crisis of the influx of Palestinian refugees into neighboring and recently independent Arab states posed huge demographic, economic, and political challenges for Egypt, Jordan, Syria, and Lebanon. A new generation of educators and relief workers, too, came into being.

My father was born into that tradition of service, which came to form almost a nationality of its own: allegiance from a distance to one's country of citizenship but allegiance equally to an adoptive land. That adoptive allegiance deepened over generations. When Dad was born in Beirut in 1931, the political landscape of the Eastern Mediterranean was in flux. The collapse of the Ottoman Empire was but thirteen years old, and the European mandates and protectorates dotting the Middle Eastern map were in awkward transition to independent statehood. In the midst of this broad transformation occurred the implantation of a Jewish population and the displacement of a Palestinian one, adding hugely to an already complex picture. And if the new Jewish state, a theocracy, posed the question of the role of religion in national life, many of its neighbors were asking similar questions. In the Muslim community,

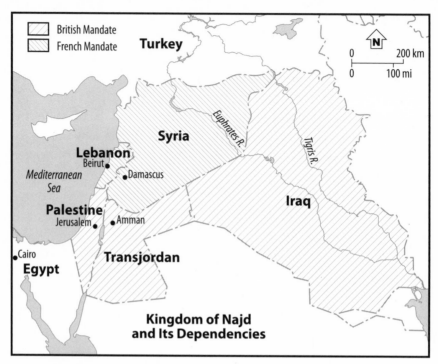

1. Eastern Mediterranean, 1931

that question involved the role of Islam in a modern, increasingly secular, world.

Dad's appointment as AUB president in 1982 marked the fulfillment of his inherited values and came at a time when the map of the Middle East was not only still transforming but crying out in full protest at its constant redrawing over centuries from the input of outsiders with outsiders' interests. Lebanon's outsiders at that time included not just Americans, French, Syrians, Israelis, and Iranians, but the United Nations multinational peacekeeping forces as well. In 1977 when my mother and I visited Lebanon, it was startling to come across a UN-capped soldier from Fiji manning a Beirut checkpoint. I wondered what the locals thought about that. Dad represented at once the outsider and the insider, both in terms of his perceptions and in the way he was perceived.

That inheritance, and its basis of human service, was Dad's driving force in his role at AUB. His professional training as a political scientist

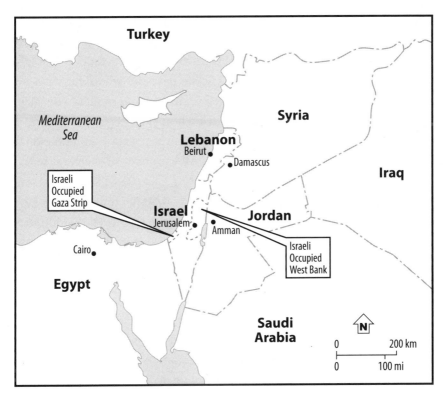

2. Eastern Mediterranean, 1984

enabled a calm and analytical view of the chaos that surrounded him. There was on a daily basis the challenge of living alongside virtually dozens of parties and points of view, not just in Lebanon or Beirut but also inside the university itself. A sense of fairness and a particular sensitivity to the disadvantaged characterized Dad's approach. Ironically, this sensitivity may have contributed to the motives for his assassination, for he didn't fit the portrait of the pushy and ignorant American who might have helped to inspire the anti-Western campaign. Yet he held on to these principles until the end, and that was a legacy that inspired in me an attitude of forgiveness and understanding, rather than equal justice through revenge.

Roy Mottahedeh's book *The Mantle of the Prophet* is a study of traditional Islamic learning in the Iranian town of Qom, a tradition out of which grew the ideas of Ayatollah Khomeini and the school of clerics who inspired the Iranian Islamic revolution.[3] For me, this book humanized Iran and the players in the Islamic revolution—a revolution that has had a profound effect on the entire Middle East and whose legacy is so directly linked to the issues on the table in today's international debates. The essence of Mottahedeh's humanization is not just the establishment of common ground but the refusal to cast any single, rigid Iranian national character. Instead, it emphasizes the natural variations of character in the human spectrum, as is found in any society.

The author states openly that his book is written on the basis of love for Iran and its history and culture. The language employed by Mottahedeh in his vibrant imparting of Iranian history is one of respect. Surely that is the only useful language in a time of need for greater knowledge and understanding of other cultures.

In his preface to a later edition, Mottahedeh makes the suggestion that, as with debates about the legacy of the French Revolution in its protracted aftermath, perhaps in the long run the enormous suffering induced by Iran's Islamic revolution will somehow be justified in the context of the long-term goal of revolutionary social change.

But can there be any basis for justifying human suffering brought about by intentional violence? For there is another form of idealism that must be upheld, one that stands alongside the honorable goals of revolutionary social change: the humane treatment of fellow human beings in every circumstance. Failure on that score cannot help but bring human civilization down to a lower rank.

Ultimately, violence must in principle be condemned. It must in and of itself be intolerable. The opportunity to carry out violence in a situation of anarchy and warfare, as seen in Lebanon and elsewhere, is an invitation not just to the politically motivated but also to what Terry Waite, a British hostage in 1980s Beirut, described in a conversation with me as the psychopathic segment that exists in every society. History shows us countless examples of this most dangerous phenomenon. Violence begets violence, and the delicate balance that maintains standards of humanity collapses quickly. The absolute condemnation of violence is an idealistic stance, but a necessary one.

It is a long way from instinctive, natural forgiveness to a strong and purposeful conviction that upholds the highest principles of humanity. One can easily forgive but then turn away and attempt to shield one's eyes from the face of evil. In order to adopt a strong conviction of humanity, one must first confront that evil and accept that one has been touched by it. I think of the rape victim who wishes to keep her horror to herself, to admit it to no one, perhaps in some kind of hope of preventing that horror from overwhelming her. To accept and admit the assault would leave her exposed and vulnerable in her mind to further attack. In practical terms, it would mean the potential of facing the rapist again, perhaps in a courtroom or in a police lineup.

When Dad was murdered, I turned away from the Middle East, a place that from earliest memory had been part of me. I could not bear to read about it or allow my grief to be touched. I felt no hatred. On the contrary, I felt profoundly helpless in the knowledge that that unseen counterpart of mine had also suffered wounds, and that both of us were the victims of political fallout. How does one bring political fallout to justice?

．　．　．

A few years after Dad's assassination, my husband's job as a China historian took us unexpectedly to England, where we settled in one of the small villages that surround the university town of Cambridge. Neither Hans nor I had any ties to this new country, and there was something both daunting and appropriate about having to make a fresh start.

To my eye, the network of villages in which we found ourselves was still organized around a traditional social structure. Although their congregations might have diminished over the years, the ancient parish churches remained central in many practical ways to the life of the larger community. They brought people together in mundane but constant ways. Dividing these villages were swaths of land wholly devoted to agriculture. Even though, in the age of modern machinery, the number of farmers required to cultivate the fields was no more than a handful, still the sight of growing crops dominated the landscape and gave anyone living among them a special awareness of the cycle of the seasons. Over many years, this environment offered me the chance for solitude in nature but also for new perspectives about people as individuals and in groups.

These were villages whose thousand-year-old Norman churches were only half as old as the villages themselves. Digging foundations for a new house might unearth Victorian glass, Roman pottery, or even Stone Age flint. I would have to laugh at the annual intervillage tug-of-war and barbecue when the victor and vanquished might, in semiseriousness, remark on some ancient village feud that had just been given new lifeblood. Family names on village war memorials were the same as those in the monthly parish newsletters that advertised local plumbers and electricians and announced the latest weddings and funerals. With a foreign surname and accent, acceptance in some quarters of my village took time.

Over a dozen years and more in this setting, I gained a greater sense of the continuum of human history and the role of the individual as both vital and barely significant. As the human continuum vastly outlives the individual, so the agricultural landscape is testimony to the supremacy of nature. We depend on nature, and yet it will do as it pleases. All this makes for a healthy sense of humility and reveals the endurance of human civilization through all its ups and downs. Gradually, with the benefit of such perspectives, my own predicament found its place in the broad scheme of things.

Perhaps even more important was that long-awaited rebirth brought on by the arrival of children, and the courage, toughness, and flexibility that children demand of their parents. This allowed, slowly at first, the creation of a new reservoir of strength: strength to plan for the future rather than just to pass the time, and strength to accept the past and to move on constructively rather than wander any which way away from it.

To inquisitive children one must explain the past, particularly when it belongs to them also, and one must state clearly what one believes to be right and wrong. One must explain how a missing grandfather died and why—and what happened next. It must all make sense. A child's pure sense of morality can push the uncertain adult to adopt a stance. Equally in that exchange, a child might express a conclusion that the adult knows to be misguided, and that must be put right.

Johan, Willem, and Derek on the Isle of Mull, Scotland, 1999.

For me, all of these thoughts and perspectives led to accepting that variation in the human spectrum: in my country of birth, in my country of residence, and in my country of citizenship. It means accepting the basic human responsibility to uphold and promote humanity in all reaches of society: at home, in one's immediate community, and in one's larger world. It means accepting the critical responsibilities of citizenship. There is in this acceptance of and sense of belonging to the common human spectrum a marvelous revelation of hope, for along with evil there is always good. In this clearer understanding of right and wrong, one sees that forgiveness is not just a soft instinct, but an essential tool in ending cycles of violence.

At the same time, forgiveness does not preclude justice. The famous photograph of the pope forgiving his would-be assassin showed the two men looking into each other's eyes, hands clasped. The gunman, it seemed, accepted as his due a period of incarceration. The victim was able to look full face at his assailant. In that meeting was the establishment of common ground, a mutual acceptance of the past and its consequences, but also a mutual determination to face the future, and in doing so to come together.

3

The Antiterrorism and Effective Death Penalty Act of 1996

ON APRIL 24, 1996, twenty-seven-year-old Andrew Kerr, now an employee of the National Security Council, sat side-by-side with former Beirut hostage Joseph Cicippio in the sunshine of the White House garden. They had been invited along with other "victims of terrorism" to witness President Clinton's signature to the groundbreaking Antiterrorism and Effective Death Penalty Act.[1]

As the makeup of Clinton's audience suggested, the Antiterrorism Act (as we came to know it) reflected a protracted and continuing period of terrorism that by its very definition involved innocent men, women, and children and their families in a whole new form of international conflict. The act was the first effort by a national government to respond to the problem as manifested on the international stage through its own judiciary.

Terrorism in domestic contexts had long been dealt with by domestic courts. Italy had developed a whole body of legislation concerning the rights of the victims of terrorism in response to the era of violence and intimidation by the Mafia, the Red Brigades, and others. In the United States, the perpetrators of the Oklahoma City bombing were prosecuted by state and federal law. The phenomenon of cross-national terrorism, however, lacked an institutional framework for legal response, and the Antiterrorism Act was a pioneering attempt to meet that need.

However, by enabling victims to take legal action in U.S. District Courts against the foreign governments responsible for sponsoring terrorist attacks, the Antiterrorism Act marked a radical departure from two hundred years of American constitutional law that prohibited U.S. courts from prosecuting cases that impinged on the immunity of foreign states. Indeed, foreign sovereign immunity was the norm in legal systems across the world. Now, U.S. legislation had broken with a fundamental and universal tradition.

Critics of the act could be found everywhere. In the eyes of the State Department and the White House, the act invaded their traditional domain of foreign policy. Indeed President Clinton was careful when he agreed to sign the act to prohibit specifically the use of frozen foreign assets in any potential compensatory damage awards to plaintiffs. In the case of Iran, whose assets were frozen in 1979 when Khomeini's Islamic revolutionaries held fifty-two staff members of the U.S. Embassy in Tehran hostage for 444 days (resulting in the severing of diplomatic relations between the two countries), frozen assets constituted a potentially useful negotiating tool in any future discussions concerning the restoration of diplomatic relations. Clinton would not let go of the bargaining chip that frozen assets represented. Therefore, while the Antiterrorism Act allowed civil claims against state perpetrators of terrorism, it provided no mechanism for funding any resulting compensation awards. If the act was designed to have a deterrent effect on terrorism by imposing large fines on its perpetrators in the form of compensation awards, it was limited, in its infancy, to symbolic gestures.

If the State Department disliked the intrusion of the judiciary into its domain of foreign affairs, it nevertheless enjoyed enormous and intrinsic authority over the implementation of the act—though this authority was tied up with still other points of contention. The act authorized claims only against so-called "state sponsors of terrorism," as designated by the U.S. secretary of state. In 1996, the list included Cuba, Iran, Iraq, Libya, North Korea, the Sudan and Syria. The glaring absence of other states known to fit the definition of a state sponsor of terrorism, by virtue of direct and systematic involvement in acts of torture, kidnapping, and assassination, rendered the act vulnerable to accusations of politics and subjectivity.

The discretion of the secretary of state in determining the contents of the list of state sponsors of terrorism was challenged on constitutional grounds. In one of the early cases brought to court by the Antiterrorism Act, *Daliberti v. Iraq* (which concerned the illegal detention in inhumane conditions of three Americans working in Kuwait), Iraq contested the case on the grounds that the discretion of the U.S. secretary of state over judicial matters, by his or her determination of the list of designated state sponsors of terrorism, was unconstitutional.[2] Numerous U.S. legal experts shared the Iraqi view.

In its fine print, the Antiterrorism Act strived for fairness and reciprocity. It upheld the right of any national judiciary to prosecute cases of international terrorism. It authorized the United States judiciary to prosecute cases of terrorism involving a U.S. citizen occurring outside its borders only if the foreign government in question neglected to take up the matter in its own courts. In other words, that foreign state was given the first option to prosecute the case. If it neglected to prosecute, then the case could be taken up in U.S. courts. In this way, the act was designed to ensure the right of the victim of terrorism to legal recourse.

However equitable these and other provisions, still the principle of domestic courts prosecuting cases of an international nature contained inherent dangers of politics and subjectivity, and ultimately, the power to protect one's own. A classic example of this point was the refusal of the U.S. to participate in the formation of the International Criminal Court, with the motive of protecting its own high officials, such as Henry Kissinger in the case of Cambodia, from accusations of war crimes.

Another example lay within the sphere of U.S.-Iran relations and underscored the U.S. government's inclination to self-protection. On July 3, 1988, the U.S. Navy guided missile cruiser USS *Vincennes* shot down Air Iran Flight 655 over the Persian Gulf, killing all 290 people on board, including 66 children. The U.S. refused to apologize for the incident or to accept any responsibility for wrongdoing. Vice President George Bush, at a news conference a month after the disaster, declared, "I will never apologize for the United States of America—I don't care what the facts are."[3]

Ultimately Iran took the matter to the International Court of Justice in The Hague (a court for which the United States recognizes jurisdiction only on a case-by-case basis). The matter was resolved in February 1996 when, in an out-of-court settlement, the U.S. government agreed to pay Iran a total of $61.9 million in compensation ($300,000 per wage-earning passenger and $150,000 per non-wage-earning passenger)—a paltry sum compared with the compensation awards that would arise for American plaintiffs filing suits under the Antiterrorism Act. The settlement was explicitly characterized as *ex gratia* by the United States, which denied any liability or responsibility for the downing of Air Iran 655.[4]

If the Antiterrorism Act's shortcomings were to be found in the broader political world in which principles of responsibility were put to the test, its own specific merits in terms of effectiveness in curtailing terrorism by nonviolent means could be proven only through practice over time. Not until July 2000 was an amendment to the act enacted that enabled the actual funding of compensation awards in a limited number of cases—putting the act into effective practice and allowing its deterrent effect to test the waters.

Amid contentious discussion over its strengths and weaknesses, the principle of the pursuit of a nonviolent response to terrorism stood out as the Antiterrorism Act's inherent merit. It was this fundamental basis of a legal and peaceful quest for accountability that began to draw the interest of those ordinary American families who had been affected by terrorism into considering the use of the act as a vehicle to formal justice.

Indeed, the need for action that the Antiterrorism Act represented came not just from a government grappling with a phenomenon that Dad himself had described in 1982 as "virulent anti-Americanism and punitive hostility," at least in the case of revolutionary Iran.[5] It reflected, too, the raw rage of some of the individual victims of that punitive hostility and their determination to do something constructive to hold the perpetrators accountable.

One such victim was Stephen Flatow, whose nineteen-year-old daughter, Alicia, had been killed in a 1995 bus bomb in Gaza by Palestinian Islamic Jihad, an organization that, like Hizballah in Lebanon, was financed by the government of Iran. Alicia, a Brandeis University student on a year abroad in Jerusalem, had boarded a bus in Jerusalem en route to a weekend at the Gaza beach resort of Gush Kalif. She was caught in PIJ's campaign against Israeli settlements. In his family's lawsuit three years later, Mr. Flatow was asked to describe the impact of his daughter's death on her mother. His reply took all of three words and explained Mrs. Flatow's absence from the courtroom. He said, "It's destroyed her."[6]

The impetus for formal action reflected, too, the release and return home of the thirteen American hostages who had survived their captivity in Lebanon and now had the freedom to rebuild their lives. By December 1991, the release of the last American hostage, Terry Anderson, had been achieved through the quiet diplomatic efforts of the UN secretary general's negotiator, Giandomenico Picco. Many French, German, Irish, and British hostages, too, had been held in Iran's anti-Western campaign and along with the American hostages constituted the large pool of captives whose release Picco had worked to gain. His work stood out in stark contrast to the arms-for-hostages deal that resulted in the release of Ben Weir in 1985 and David Jacobsen and Martin Jenco in 1986, before its cover was blown. The debacle resulted in the stalling of any diplomatic efforts to secure the release of the remaining hostages.

Picco's book *Man Without a Gun* describes his extraordinary maneuvering, largely between the U.S. and Iranian governments, and the promises that he extracted from each side toward the release of the Western hostages.[7] In the end, not long after Anderson's release in December 1991 but with two German hostages still captive, Picco was forced to resign his position when the United States reneged on a promise to make a goodwill gesture to Iran (such as polite phraseology in a prominent speech), in response to the latter's influence upon the Hizballah kidnappers to effect the release of the Americans in the group. George Bush Senior's administration decided that it could not, as promised to Picco three years earlier when it was desperate to secure the release of its hostages, be seen to have made any sort of deal with Iran. Picco's credibility in Tehran was destroyed, and he had no choice but to resign. His overall success on behalf of Secretary General Pérez de Cuéllar never received media headlines and yet marked an enormous diplomatic achievement by the United Nations.

As the hostages regained their freedom, some found that the rebuilding of their lives depended upon the pursuit of formal justice, even though in the early 1990s no appropriate legal framework existed. In 1993, Joseph Cicippio and David Jacobsen, formerly of AUB, and Frank Reed, formerly of Beirut's International College, all of whom were tortured and held hostage in Lebanon over a period of years, together brought forward a case against the government of Iran. The presiding judge told the plaintiffs that as horrific as the crimes against them were, there was nothing the court could do. When the Antiterrorism Act was passed, Cicippio, Jacobsen, and Reed again came forward collectively, and theirs was the first hostage case to move successfully through the courts. A judgment on their behalf against the government of Iran was secured in 1998.[8]

Terry Anderson, the former Associated Press bureau chief in Beirut, was another hostage determined to seek formal justice, whose case followed the *Cicippio* judgment. Anderson's career background in reporting and journalism added another dimension to his quest. He told me that while he felt compelled to tell his kidnappers "you can't do that," he was driven first to acquire as much information as possible about the circumstances surrounding his seven-year captivity. Within a year of his release, he returned to Lebanon as a researcher on his own case and interviewed a range of key Hizballah members. Back in the United States, he began the lengthy process of seeking the declassification of intelligence documents pertaining to his case under the Freedom of Information Act (FOIA). So intractable was the bureaucratic jungle of FOIA that Anderson found a law firm, Crowell and Moring, willing to assist him in this task on a pro bono basis. The early results of his research were published in his memoir, *Den of Lions.*[9] Further investigations contributed to the presentation of evidence in his case against the government of Iran in February 2000.[10]

As with the range of emotional response to bereavement inside one close family, so the Beirut hostages—who in many cases had spent years locked and chained alongside one another, with endless time to discuss the ethical dimensions of their predicament—responded in various ways to the possibility of formal justice as offered by the Antiterrorism Act. For a variety of reasons having to do with the tremendous and preoccupying challenge of reuniting with families and with an altered world, most did not immediately come forward to employ the legislation.

Benjamin Weir was a Presbyterian minister who had worked among the Shi'ites of Lebanon for more than thirty years prior to his kidnapping. A spiritual mentor to Cicippio, Jacobsen, Reed, and Anderson in captivity, Weir lived through eighteen years of newfound freedom before he came to the conclusion that the pursuit of formal justice via the Antiterrorism Act was a step he wished to take. He had waited a long time, he explained, for Iran to make a gesture to acknowledge acceptance of responsibility for its actions.[11]

Similarly, David Dodge, a son and grandson of AUB presidents and a man who had spent much of his life in Lebanon, was kidnapped from the AUB campus in 1982 but did not embark on legal action until twenty years after his release.[12] It must be said that by and large, the victims of Iran's anti-Western campaign were idealistic people who were engaged in professions oriented to service. They were experienced professionals who could have worked anywhere but had chosen Lebanon. They were targeted because they were easy to strike. The paths they pursued in pursuit of legal justice were characteristically idealistic. For some this meant many years' reflection while for others it meant an instinctive determination to seek formal justice.

While the instinct for formal justice was not universally shared in the years immediately following their release, many found catharsis through writing. Many former hostages wrote their memoirs, both in the United States and in Europe, and I read as many as I could. One, *An Evil Cradling,* by the Irish hostage Brian Keenan, joined the ranks of classic studies of captivity.[13] His and other memoirs spelled out the details of a fantasy I had nurtured on and off for nearly eight years: that Dad had in fact been among the hostages and would come home to us one day. I was fascinated by the details of the hostages' existence that I had often imagined Dad enduring, and as I read I would evaluate his chances of surviving that experience. I imagined him as a student in Tom Sutherland's makeshift dairy farming course, or indulging in chess with Terry Anderson. Other members of my family confessed to the same thoughts, and we agreed that Dad would most definitely have survived the experience—though admittedly, in our fanciful imaginations, we did not like to include images of Dad sick and being forced to excrete into filthy plastic bags, beaten for a defiant remark, or mummy-wrapped in masking tape, riding in a coffin-shaped box under a moving truck en route to some new underground prison . . .

What came as a surprise in the course of this reading was not the descriptions of the horrific circumstances of captivity in underground cells, coffins, and chains, with its attendant demons of claustrophobia, suffocation, and the threat of insanity. Instead, it was a footnote on page 54 of Terry Anderson's *Den of Lions,* which spelled out certain details of the planning and carrying out of the assassination of Malcolm Kerr. Anderson wrote,

> The assassination of Kerr was a carefully planned operation of Hizballah. Kerr was labeled a "dangerous spy" by Ali's Centre, the central data bank on foreigners in Beirut. A woman agent was sent to smuggle a gun in her purse into the American University campus. The gun was buried beside a tree near College Hall [and Dad's ashes were later buried beside a tree near College Hall]. It remained until an official *fatwa,* or religious ruling, was issued by Hizballah's central council condemning Kerr to death. On January 18, 1984, two male agents were sent to carry out the sentence, shooting Kerr twice in the head at close range. He died immediately. The two assassins fled without hindrance.[14]

The next footnote on the same page describes the case of William Buckley, the CIA's Beirut station chief, who was kidnapped in March of the same year. According to Anderson,

> The Hizballah operation against Buckley was almost a model of counterespionage. Buckley had developed a woman Shiite agent named Zeynoub [*sic*], sister of the woman involved in the assassination of American University President Kerr. Unknown to him, she was a double, a "responsible," or official in Hizballah, whose true loyalty was with the fundamentalist party. According to one usually reliable source, Buckley grew enamored of the woman and began an affair with her. Later, however, the professional CIA man began to grow suspicious. Before he decided to act on those suspicions, the woman became aware of them. With the information she now had, and access to his apartment, the kidnapping was easy. The decision to take him was made on Friday, March 15, 1984. On March 16, in an operation involving twelve cars full of Hizballah agents, he was snatched.[15]

Following his kidnapping, Buckley was apparently tortured over a period of fourteen months under the supervision of one Imad Mughniyeh, until he weakened and died. His death rattle was heard by David Jacobsen and Terry Anderson, whose underground cells were adjacent to Buckley's.[16] Reading this yanked me out of any fantasy that Dad might have been a hostage. Instead I thanked God that the gun purported to have been hidden under that tree near College Hall had been used with such precision as to cause his instantaneous death.

Terry Anderson's book was published in 1993, three years before the enactment of the Antiterrorism Act. I read it in 1994, the tenth anniversary year of Dad's death. Whether or not it was true, the infamous footnote was the first published allegation concerning the identity of Dad's killers that had come to our attention—notwithstanding, of course, media reports following his assassination. I was fascinated as to how Anderson had obtained the information. Ten years later he served as an expert witness in our own lawsuit against the government of Iran and explained his methodology: in short, he had applied the rules of newspaper journalism, in which at least two independent and verifiable sources were obtained to confirm the same piece of information. Both sources had come from under the umbrella of Hizballah intelligence. In the years that followed the publication of his book, the information had never been refuted, although Anderson had regularly asked his wide range of contacts to challenge his findings.

The graphic nature of Anderson's footnote was chilling and caught my imagination. The whole notion of intelligence gathering and careful planning of an assassination by a variety of people, from official policy makers to hit men, rocked my vague and somehow sympathetic image of a downtrodden individual driven to madness. For the first time, I was tempted to explore the question of the identity of Dad's murderers. However, by opening the door even a crack, I was allowing new and unknown elements to filter into my carefully protected world.

I opened up the large cardboard box in the attic labeled "Dad's Papers" and lost myself in them. I would spend hours staring at his broken glasses and the minute residue of blackened, dried blood embedded in the broken point on the horn rim. I'd put the glasses on (each time having to

Dad addressing the Foreign Policy Association, circa 1983.

reinsert one of the lenses into the broken frame) and bask blurrily in some strange kind of closeness to Dad. Then I would dart wildly among the papers. I found the thick, cream-colored *In Memoriam* order of service from the Nassau Presbyterian Church in Princeton, New Jersey, with Dad's gentle face gracing the cover. I found Dad's last letter to me, written on January 16, 1984, admonishing me in jest about the $17.50 I owed him for the cost of the Graduate Record Exam, which I planned to take that year. I found all the clippings saved by my grandmother Elsa, who had borne so silently the unnatural loss of her beloved son. I found lots of black-and-white photographs of Dad giving speeches and meeting dignitaries that he would have made funny remarks about: enjoying a chat with Senator William Fulbright at some Washington cocktail party, sitting with David Dodge and Najeeb Halaby in Senator Charles Percy's office, standing next to my mother and shaking hands with Lebanese president Elias Sarkis, seated casually on a sofa next to Yasser Arafat (also in Beirut), and my favorite—dashingly handsome Dad addressing the Foreign Policy Association in the really good old days.

There were many newspaper and magazine articles in the box that I had never read: several from the Beirut weekly *Monday Morning*, and one from a right-wing Washington newspaper called *The Spotlight*, which made breathtaking allegations of Israeli collaboration with Lebanese Shi'ites in the kidnapping of David Dodge. All were fascinating but mysterious, because long ago I had slammed the door to reading anything about Lebanon and therefore had no basis of knowledge upon which to judge the material now before me. I could not analyze or discriminate or even digest what I read. And yet with Terry Anderson's tantalizing footnote, I felt suddenly obsessed with the question of who had killed Dad. I honestly wondered if the answer might lie hidden in the depths of this very cardboard box!

It was fortunate that the obsession came to a sudden end, for it made me nearly forget my real life. Hans and I were now the proud parents of two beautiful little boys, Johan and Derek, and had at last found a meaningful route forward. I wrote to David Dodge, whom Dad had visited shortly after his release, and asked if he could enlighten me in any way on the subject of Dad's death. He had been held by Hizballah in Lebanon and then imprisoned in Iran itself, and perhaps, I thought, he would know something about Dad's murderers. His gentle but firm response to me was that surely the important thing now was to live life and to focus on the future rather than on the past. Exhausted and with a sense of relief, I put the cardboard box back into the attic.

While I had fished around so fleetingly and inexpertly, Andrew had never closed the door to knowledge and information. Conversely, he had developed a detailed understanding of the makings of the death trap into which Dad had walked back in 1984. Incredibly, even if he had lost so much of the memory of his life with his father, he had developed a broad understanding of Lebanese history and the politics of the 1980s before which the rest of the family stood in awe.

The basis of Andrew's information came from conventional reading. But his appointment to the Situation Room at the National Security Council—his first job upon graduation from the University of Arizona in 1992—put him in the position of access to sophisticated information emanating from the U.S. government intelligence apparatus. In the course of his work, the purpose of which was to direct incoming data to the appropriate desks at the NSC, he became highly knowledgeable of the affairs of Lebanon and the Middle East.

A year or so into this job, his knowledge of Lebanon was supplemented dramatically by a shocking piece of information. Quite inadvertently, Andrew stumbled upon a document that brought to light both a person who claimed to have ensured the firing of the gun that had killed Dad, and a person who apparently needed to know that the deed had been done. It suggested that the assassination had been commissioned and approved by senior authorities in the Hizballah apparatus, which included officials of the Iranian government. Andrew's experience at the NSC gave him the ability to judge the credibility of this three-page document, and he knew he could not dismiss its contents. So highly classified was the information that the document would never be released under the Freedom of Information Act, and the rest of us have never seen it.

Such was Andrew's professionalism that he did not share his knowledge of the document with anyone. However, in his remaining years at the NSC, the essence of what he had stumbled upon was repeated and confirmed in various documents that crossed his desk in the course of his work. Years later, it was further confirmed to us by Robert Oakley, a former State Department director of counterterrorism who, of course, would have been privy to the same damning document Andrew had come across.

In Oakley's view, Iran, in its role as political and financial patron of the Hizballah organization, had sponsored Dad's assassination.

When I first heard of the full name of the Antiterrorism Act, which is "The Antiterrorism and Effective Death Penalty Act," I instantly and naïvely assumed that it dealt with the wrongfulness of death sentences per se. The act's phrasing, "effective death penalty," made me jump, for certainly Dad's death penalty had been carried out effectively. Of course I was wildly mistaken, and felt sickened when I understood that the act in fact contained provisions for the effective implementation of the death penalty inside the United States. For practical reasons, the issues of international terrorism and the death penalty in certain American states had been dealt with in one legislative package, hence the title of the act. But the irony was quite difficult to swallow: I knew that my own moral stance against terrorism was not just about the victimization of innocent people, but also about the fundamental sanctity of human life. Even as a child I felt an innate and powerful conviction that death as official punishment had no place in a society that strove for the highest standards of humane conduct.

The arrival of the Antiterrorism Act on Clinton's desk took Andrew by surprise. Unexpectedly, he had been privy to the details of his father's assassination, and yet at the same time he was unaware of the legislative process in Congress that was at work to produce the Antiterrorism Act. Soon came the invitation to witness Clinton's signature to the act in April 1996. While Andrew was, along with other members of the audience that day, an "ordinary" victim of terrorism, he was also a member of the president's own staff, and as such was mentioned in Clinton's speech:

> I'd like to close with a word to all of the family members of Americans slain by terrorists and to the survivors of terrorism, to the children who lost their parents in Pan Am 103 and parents who lost their children in Israel, to all of you from Oklahoma City, to Andrew Kerr on my staff of the National Security Council whose father was murdered in Beirut, to each and every one of you with us today and those who are watching across this great land of ours. Your endurance and your courage is a lesson to us all.[17]

I asked Andrew if Clinton actually knew him by sight, and Andrew laughed and said no. In the receiving line after the ceremony, Andrew was introduced to the president, who said, "So *you're* Andrew Kerr!"

For Andrew, this was a momentous day to say the least. Once he had been a fifteen-year-old boy who dreamed of avenging his father's death according to the age-old adage of an eye for an eye, a tooth for a tooth. Now he was a thoughtful young man armed with knowledge and a legal process at his disposal. An opportunity lay before him to seek formal justice and, at last, to do something in his father's name.

4

The Decision to Take Legal Action

ONE WINTRY DAY at the end of 2002, nearly seven years after Clinton's signature to the Antiterrorism Act and just three weeks before our trial against the government of Iran, I paid a visit to Terry Waite in his beautiful, ancient cottage near the East Anglian town of Bury St. Edmunds. I had written to him in conjunction with my research for our trial, and although he confessed in his letter of reply that he had no specific information about Dad, still we arranged to meet and talk. As with other former Beirut hostages, I felt a strange bond of experience in spite of the fact that we had never met.

Terry had been the archbishop of Canterbury's envoy in the early and mid-1980s, commissioned with the task of negotiating the release of hostages in Iran, Libya, and Lebanon. When the archbishop was approached by the family of Hizballah hostage Reverend Benjamin Weir, Waite became involved in negotiations with Weir's captors, resulting, or so it seemed, in the eventual release of three hostages: Weir, David Jacobsen, and Father Martin Jenco. The subsequent exposure of the arms-for-hostages affair undermined Waite's credibility as a Western negotiator, and during a later attempt to bring about the release of remaining Hizballah-held hostages, Waite himself was taken captive. He spent four years in solitary confinement, and a fifth in the company of Terry Anderson, Tom Sutherland, and fellow-Briton John McCarthy.

Now we sat by the fire in his sitting room, where he showed me the books he was currently reading, as well as some lovely wooden beams dating back five hundred years. The smell of roast chicken came wafting in from the oil-burning stove in the kitchen nearby. This was Terry's retreat, where at the moment he was writing a book about solitude. He struck me at once as a busy and contented man, and one who wasted no precious time on bitterness or regret over five lost years.

I quizzed him about the Beirut of his day, hoping to glean any information that might contribute to my emerging composite sketch of the environment in which Dad had been assassinated. What I had not appreciated until this quiet conversation was the wider meaning of anarchy in wartime, always looking instead for specific, clear-cut explanations for Dad's killing. As Terry had discovered from experience, anarchy presents the opportunity for psychopathic behavior, adding an important element to the already complex mixture of forces at work in 1980s Beirut.

Then Terry asked me about our decision to take legal action against the Iranian government. Why had we initiated a lawsuit? As I tried to explain, I detected a bemused curiosity in his expression. I couldn't help feeling envious of the peaceful, private circumstances in which I found him, and the fact that British victims of terrorism such as he had no such decisions to make, since Britain and the European Union lacked provisions for lawsuits against foreign governments. I wondered what his decision would have been had he been in my shoes.

While some found our decision curious, others were baffled as to why it had taken us so long to come forward and seek justice in Dad's name. In Beirut, where my mother spent the summer of 2001 teaching summer school at AUB, former colleagues of my parents and grandparents could not understand why we should not seek formal justice. Law and order had been absent in wartime Beirut, and thousands of murders and kidnappings had gone unprosecuted. For us, as citizens of a country with a functioning legal system, it was considered only natural to let that judiciary address the ultimate injustice.

The provision available to us was a civil lawsuit, in which the onus is on the individual, rather than on the state, to initiate and pursue legal action. While the Antiterrorism Act empowered victims of terrorism by providing the opportunity for legal recourse, it also presented for some a nearly impossible challenge. For an ordinary family to confront the government of another country over the politically loaded subject of terrorism is an extraordinary exercise. It involves among other things the complexity of the family itself as it is forced into unified decision making, reliving the event in question, and issues of evidence, compensation, and political and ethical principles.

Although I found it difficult to answer Terry Waite's question—why initiate a lawsuit?—I found it equally difficult to answer the question put forth by our old Beirut friends—why not?

The decision to file a lawsuit followed no clear or logical path. It evolved over time and demanded a constant thrashing out of difficult issues. The spectacular compensation likely to be awarded to us by the U.S. District Court, even if never to come to fruition, somehow encompassed a whole host of dilemmas and stood in our path from the very beginning.

■ ■ ■

Around the time of my visit to Terry Waite, a United States District Judge by the name of Paul Friedman issued his opinion on the case of Beverly Surette, the widow of William Buckley, versus the Islamic Republic of Iran. Buckley's death as a hostage of Hizballah on June 3, 1985, brought an end to the torture and deprivation of medical care to which he had been subjected since his kidnapping in March 1984. Judge Friedman awarded Surette ten million dollars in damages, acknowledging that "while no amount of money could ever truly compensate Ms. Surette for the agony she has suffered, the Court finds this to be a fair award, consistent with the relief awarded in similar cases by other judges of this Court."[1] The fact that William Buckley's widow did not actually receive that ten million dollars in compensation, since no funding mechanism existed for the payment of her award, added to its symbolic nature.

The symbolic importance of compensation for pain and suffering, and the difficulty of putting a price on it, is universally recognized. China still awaits compensation from Japan, sixty years after Japan's brutal occupation of its mainland neighbor. The act of paying compensation is a powerfully symbolic gesture, which embodies public recognition of wrongdoing by the offender and, for the victim, acknowledgment of what some European countries call "moral damage" and "violation of personal integrity."[2] The American legal term is "solatium," meaning "comfort in distress," or "compensation for wounded feelings."

Earlier compensation awards to victims of Iranian-sponsored terrorism in Lebanon—seven, to be exact—had gone beyond symbolism and had been paid out to plaintiffs by means of a funding mechanism set out in the July 2000 Justice for Victims of Terrorism Act. By the terms of this legislation, the U.S. Treasury acted as a subrogation agent and paid out compensation awards against specifically earmarked frozen Iranian assets. The expectation was that eventually, the Treasury would recover its costs by drawing from those assets. The Justice for Victims of Terrorism Act deliberately confined the number of cases eligible for compensation payment by imposing a closing date, in order to test the waters. The last case to be paid was that of the estate of Father Martin Jenco on August 2, 2001. The so-called second generation of cases filed after the deadline would lack a funding mechanism.

Beyond these seven cases were three cases of Iranian-sponsored terrorism in Israel, one of Iranian-sponsored terrorism in Paris, three of Cuban-sponsored terrorism, and three of Iraqi-sponsored terrorism, bringing the total to seventeen cases. Cuban cases were funded against Cuban frozen assets, and Iraqi cases against Iraqi frozen assets.

In addition to solatium for the victim and his or her immediate family, plaintiffs in civil suits brought to the U.S. District Court under the Antiterrorism Act were awarded compensation for loss of income, captivity, torture, and suffering from physical wounds. Just as a formula of sorts had evolved for calculations of solatium, so formulas evolved for calculations of these other categories. Captivity was price-tagged at ten thousand dollars per day. Torture carried a special premium, as did any period of suffering between the infliction of injury and death. Long-term kidnapping tended to draw higher compensation than murder. Indeed, strange disparities emerged—as Andrew pointed out, there was no price tag for attending a funeral—but lawyers dismissed these as inevitable vagaries of the legal system, akin to the scenario of a car accident in which long-term injuries tend to cost insurance companies more than outright deaths.

The most shocking vagary, as I saw it, related not to disparities in sums of money, but in the absence altogether of a category for loss of life. In the case of someone killed outright, all the by-products of death would be compensated, but denial of the victim's life would not. If the victim were held captive but uninjured for a day or two prior to death, the estate would be awarded ten thousand dollars per day of captivity on the basis of time withheld from freedom. If a victim survived for a period of hours between the infliction of injury and death, then the estate would be awarded compensation of up to one or two million dollars for the victim's suffering. This compensation was carefully and painfully worked out in the case of Alicia Flatow, who survived, barely conscious, for five hours after the bombing of the Israeli bus on which she was a passenger in 1994. For those like Dad who did not suffer from their wounds, and who were never held captive, there was no compensation beyond projected loss of income. That the concept of loss of life itself—the centerpiece of human rights—had not worked its way into the legal system was an incredible ethical shortcoming in the evolution of the Antiterrorism Act.

Nevertheless, all of these components of compensation more or less adhered to international legal standards. They were the norm in countries of the European Union, where they had been put into widespread effect in the aftermath of World War II. Over a period of fifty years, postwar Germany had paid out over sixty billion dollars to victims of Nazi crimes.[3] Compensation was the goal of certain countries in Africa, South America, and South Asia that lacked functioning judiciaries or where truth commissions had been given mandates to establish the foundations of justice for victims of political violence. Usually in such countries, resources for compensation were nonexistent, but occasionally compensation was paid to victims by new governments who assumed the debts of their predecessors. In Argentina, fifteen thousand families of persons who disappeared during the military regime of 1976–83 were compensated a lump sum of $220,000 each, in the form of state bonds. Children of the disappeared received, until the age of twenty-one, a monthly payment of $140. The total cost of this compensation program to the new government was between two and three billion dollars.[4]

Compensation awards made under the Antiterrorism Act were at the very top of the scale. They were so great that after pulling some families out of genuine financial hardship on account of years away from work and difficulties in re-entering the job market, some plaintiffs established large charitable foundations out of the excess of their awards.

The Sutherland family established a foundation dedicated to enriching community life in Colorado through education, social services, and the arts.[5] Terry Anderson set up the Father Lawrence Martin Jenco Foundation, in memory of his late fellow hostage, the stated purpose of which is "to recognize and support individuals who are working for the dignity and sense of worth of the people of Appalachia."[6] In 2002 the foundation's annual award went to an Appalachian homeless shelter. More of Anderson's compensation award was spent on a variety of educational projects, including scholarships in Lebanon and a long-term school building program in Vietnam, where Anderson had served as a U.S. Marine in the 1960s. However cathartic this charitable work may have been for its patrons, and however beneficial to its recipients, the money that made it possible was only a by-product of a political scheme designed for the very different purpose of hurting state governments involved in the business of sponsoring terrorism.

Later, in the case of victims of the September 11 attacks, a more modest compensation program would be designed. Because the alleged culprits could not be identified as agents of any government, the terms of the Antiterrorism Act would not apply. Therefore an entirely different scheme was designed, the purpose of which was to provide necessary financial assistance to victims' families. Under this paymaster scheme, the United States Treasury would make one-time payments averaging $1.6 million for death and between $250,000 and $6 million for injury. For death claims, this amounted essentially to at least a comfortable annual lifetime pension. Even though the scheme did not require courtroom action or a high burden of proof, by August 2003 most eligible families had neglected to take the steps necessary for the collection of the compensation to which they were entitled. The reasons for inaction were numerous, but one was that victims' families found it emotionally premature to face reliving the trauma that such a step would require.[7]

Although for some prospective plaintiffs covered under the Antiterrorism Act the statute of limitations was sensitive to their emotional needs (allowing as it did the filing of lawsuits until 2006), the huge scale of compensation was morally so uncomfortable as to impede our decision to go forward. This discomfort was rooted in the knowledge that victims of similar crimes in poor countries usually stood little chance of any form of compensation at all. John was continually haunted by this thought. Further discomfort stemmed from the knowledge that the size of the American compensation award was dictated by political motives. The very nature of the terrorism that killed Dad was such that neat delineations of guilt and innocence between disputing governments was impossible, and so the prospect of compensation within a broad and complex political scheme was deeply distressing.

We tried to deal with some of these misgivings by excluding specific sums of money from our official complaint, requesting instead that the judge appointed to our case award what we termed "appropriate compensation"—even though we knew full well that the compensation formulas that had evolved over time would still most likely serve as a basis for calculating our awards.

The other chief component of the award made in the Buckley case was punitive damages, which, unlike the concept of compensatory damages, was not universally recognized. The concept of punitive damages is an American legal invention, the purpose of which is literally to punish the perpetrator by inflicting crippling fines. Punitive damages signaled the essential intent of the Antiterrorism Act, which was to make terrorism expensive.

The punitive damage award recommended by Judge Friedman in the Buckley case again followed benchmarks established in previous cases, and was calculated by a formula that spoke directly to the act in question: the calculation was up to three times the defendants' perceived annual budget for "terrorism" during the relevant time period. The court's expert witness estimated that at the time of Buckley's incarceration and death, the Iranian government's Revolutionary Guard Corps and the Iranian Ministry of Information and Security spent "approximately $100 million each year in support of the operations of Hizballah and its terrorist activities." Therefore the punitive damage award to Buckley's family was set at $300 million. The threat of such costs to the Iranian government was hoped, as Judge Friedman stated in his opinion, to have a deterrent effect: "While the court cannot hope to end . . . unconscionable acts by the entry of a single judgment, the award of punitive damages in this case is both appropriate and necessary to punish defendants, if not to deter similar conduct in the future."[8]

The means for putting this deterrent into practice was for the U.S. government to purchase the punitive damage award from the plaintiff (at a cost of 4 percent of the plaintiff's compensatory damage award), and to insist upon the collection of the sum from the Iranian government at such time as the U.S. and Iran went to the negotiating table to discuss the normalization of diplomatic relations. This transaction, like the payment of compensation awards, depended upon the existence of a funding mechanism such as the one provided by the Justice for Victims of Terrorism Act, so that the 4 percent fee could be paid out to plaintiffs. Ultimately, the collection of punitive damages was linked directly to the restoration of diplomatic relations between former adversaries.

While the principle of punitive damages was not recognized outside the American legal system, neither was it universally endorsed inside the United States. We disliked the concept because it threatened to cripple a second generation and thus prolong enmity between nations. In the early twentieth century, for example, indemnities born out of the Boxer Rebellion crippled the Chinese economy for generations. A further argument against punitive damages was that if they were not internationally recognized, they could not serve as a common denominator in the effort to build international legal standards in response to terrorism. That the court itself was not in agreement on the issue was evident in the case of *Roeder v. Iran,* when in March 2003 Judge Emmet Sullivan ruled against an award of punitive damages.[9] Further rulings against punitive damages were made in the Regier and Dammarell cases that followed.[10]

Whether or not to include punitive damages in a civil lawsuit was a decision every plaintiff had to make. Our lawyers would stress time and again that it was "up to us," but we found it difficult to agree on the issue. My mother was firmly against the idea from the very beginning but had no difficulty understanding the feelings of those who supported it. She often wondered if, had the circumstances of Dad's death been more horrific—had he been tortured or left badly injured—she would have felt differently.

Time would prove the success of punitive damages as a deterrent tool. A limited effect was evident in 2001 and 2002 when Iran watchers reported that the enactment of the Antiterrorism Act provoked consternation and debate in the Iranian Parliament over possible financial ramifications of punitive damage awards. However, as time passed, no curb in Iranian state-sponsored terrorism could be claimed. On the contrary, if Iranian state-sponsored terrorist activities decreased in Lebanon for a time (and that probably had more to do with Hizballah's desire to transform into a mainstream political party), they increased in the West Bank and later, in postwar Iraq.

Libya, on the other hand, presented a clearer example of the success of financial pressure working to curb state sponsorship of terrorism. A combination of high compensation awards in American and French courts and UN sanctions worked to bring Libya out of the business of terrorism.

Libya's sponsorship of terrorism had included the bombing of a Pan Am flight over Lockerbie, Scotland, in December 1988, and the bombing of French UTA flight 772 over Niger in 1989, in which seven Americans were among the dead. In the case of the UTA flight, a French criminal court eventually tried two suspects, with the cooperation of the Libyan government. The suspects were found guilty and given prison sentences, and the Libyan government paid compensation to the families of the UTA crash victims. The affair reached resolution when President Jacques Chirac and Colonel Muammar Qaddafi agreed to resume diplomatic relations. Qaddafi's concern was financial, since diplomatic isolation resulting from Libya's involvement in terrorism meant the exclusion of Libya from international trade.

There were lesser-known incidents of Libyan-sponsored terrorism, including the purchase by Libya of three American and British hostages from their Hizballah captors, at a price of $1 million each, and their subsequent executions, apparently in retaliation for the American bombing of Tripoli in April 1986. The American warplanes had taken off from British soil. Two of the three executed hostages were employees of AUB and had been my parents' colleagues in the fall of 1984: Peter Kilburn, an American, had been the university librarian, and Leigh Douglas, a Briton, had been a member of the English language faculty. Years later, Kilburn's brother Blake brought a lawsuit under the Antiterrorism Act against both Iran and Libya.[11]

Although cases against the government of Iran invariably went into default status on account of Iran's rejection of the validity of U.S. courts to try them, the Libyan government participated fully in cases against its government. In the Kilburn case, Libya sent a defense team to the U.S. District Courthouse in Washington where it did not deny responsibility for carrying out the act in question but challenged the claims on grounds of due process. The court rejected the challenge, and the Libyan defense team continued to participate in the legal process. Similarly, in early 2004 the Lockerbie affair reached resolution by virtue of Qaddafi's agreement to pay compensation to victims' families.[12]

The Kilburn case, along with the Lockerbie and UTA bombings, is important because it illustrates the complex international nature of many incidents of state-sponsored terrorism and points to the need for common, cooperative strategies. It shows that in some cases, financial pressure on state sponsors of terrorism can be effective.

Meanwhile, as cases passed through the U.S. District Court, a body of evidence about state-sponsored terrorism developed. Law firms representing victims of terrorism established small archives—mostly declassified intelligence documents retrieved under the Freedom of Information Act, but also scholarly studies, which began to emerge in the 1990s. They acquired further knowledge from a collection of expert witnesses, some who were hired by law firms on a regular basis owing to what lawyers viewed as the vital nature of their expertise. Among these experts were Robert Oakley, who as the State Department's chief of counterterrorism in the mid-1980s was able to extrapolate on intelligence documents presented in court, and Patrick Clawson, an Iran expert at the Washington Institute for Near East Policy whose testimony on Iranian annual budgets for terrorism, correct or not, was instrumental in calculating punitive damage awards.

There developed a growing understanding by a community of American lawyers and potential plaintiffs of the nature of Iranian government-sponsored terrorism in Lebanon, as well as a growing sense of responsibility to address the problem. A snowball effect occurred, and those families long reluctant to become engaged in the complexities of legal action found that path increasingly hard to ignore. If finally they decided to venture down it, often they discovered that vital documentation relating to their case had already been gathered in the context of research on others. The Buckley case, for example, saw the declassification of a CIA document produced in conjunction with the search for the missing William Buckley, which identified the culprits in the murder of Malcolm Kerr.[13]

．　■　■

On July 26, 2001, one month before Andrew, my mother, and I visited the London office of Crowell and Moring for an introductory meeting with prospective lawyers Michael Martinez and Stuart Newberger, the European Commission issued its *Report on the Role of the European Union in Combating Terrorism.* The report declared that "the fight against terrorism is one of the major challenges facing us in the 21st century."[14] Its author, British Liberal Democrat Member of the European Parliament Graham Watson, emphasized that this challenge demanded cooperative international action, including legislation.

In this spirit of cooperative thinking, and with expertise gained from representing a growing number of plaintiffs in U.S. courts, Crowell and Moring responded to an appeal by the European Commission for comments and discussion in conjunction with the publication of the Report on Terrorism's derivative *Green Paper on Compensation to Crime Victims.*[15]

The response that the firm submitted in October 2001, authored by Michael Martinez, summarized the way in which the Antiterrorism Act had been applied since its enactment in April 1996.[16] It stressed in particular the motive of "making terrorism expensive" through the imposition of large fines in the form of damage awards against state sponsors of terrorism. That Crowell and Moring had taken the initiative to engage in this exchange with the EU, at a time when the U.S. government was officially opposed to the creation of an International Criminal Court, showed us in a real and practical way how individual victims of terrorism might have at least a small voice in the international discussion on response to state-sponsored terrorism. It brought a major American law firm into the sphere of EU policymaking, ensuring one form of exchange of ideas across the Atlantic.

The language of the EU's *Report* and its derivative *Green Paper* was steeped in the human-rights tradition of the EU charter. This tradition was manifested in the state's unquestioned responsibility to the individual and thus its automatic role as subrogation agent for the payment of compensation to victims of terrorist and other crimes, should such payment by the offender not be possible.

However, while the European premise of human rights was deeply rooted, the *Report on the Role of the European Union* openly acknowledged the nascent stage of thinking on the problem of response to terrorism. It pointed out that only four of fifteen EU member states—Spain, France, the UK, and Portugal—had at that point adopted definitions of the term *terrorism*, and furthermore that "these definitions differ considerably in wording and scope." The report offered its own working definition of terrorism:

A terrorist act means: "any offence committed by individuals or groups resorting to violence or threatening to use violence against a country, its institutions, its population in general or specific individuals which, being motivated by separatist aspirations, extremist ideological exceptions, fanaticism or irrational and subjective factors, is intended to create a climate of terror among official authorities, certain individuals or groups in society, or the general public."[17]

That European definitions of terrorism were varied and still only emerging was true in spheres both in and outside of government. Axa Insurance, one of Europe's largest household insurers, published a "Terrorism Exclusion" clause for its household insurance policy holders in May 2003, resting on a definition of terrorism that reflected the public hysteria of the day. Its narrow focus on the use of biological, chemical, or nuclear attacks meant that it overlooked, and therefore excluded, the torture, hostage taking, assassination, and aircraft-related disasters—including the Lockerbie crash that had destroyed both lives and household property—that had brought terrorism into global prominence. I was intrigued when my own insurance policy was renewed under these terms.

Further indications of this nascent stage of thinking could be seen in the EU's central strategy outlined for addressing the problem of terrorism. This strategy was to thwart acts of terrorism by restricting the free movement of terrorist cells within Europe. It depended on cooperation between police and judiciaries in EU member states. But like the American financially based deterrent strategy, the EU strategy was limited to preventative action. While that was doubtless vital, still it did not probe the root causes of terrorism.

Finally, the EU's *Report* amounted only to recommendations, rather than legislation. Still ahead lay the daunting task of aligning existing policies of the individual EU member states—a microcosm of the challenge of creating international standards on response to terrorism.

Whatever the limitations of the EU approach and the Antiterrorism Act, a common denominator of nonviolent response was nevertheless clearly articulated. The premise of human dignity and social responsibility, especially prominent in the European tradition, was for us a compelling one. It held a sense of promise not only for the rehabilitation of the victim, but also for the possibility of an open-minded approach to understanding and addressing the root causes of terrorism.

■   ■   ■

While these policies and laws were being drafted and tested in Europe and America, truth commissions continued to carry out their work in dozens of countries throughout South America, Africa, and South Asia. In nations stripped of the infrastructure of traditional justice that Europe and America took for granted—police, judiciaries, prisons, and sound treasuries—the most basic human needs in the aftermath of acts that my own society would have termed terrorism, but that elsewhere were termed "political violence" and "human rights abuse," stood out in stark relief.

In spite of their limited resources, the work of truth commissions was in many ways innovative and had much to offer the Western judiciaries to which some aspired. Indeed, one such contribution was the use of language. The problem of defining terrorism, as identified in the EU's *Report*, was symptomatic of its inherently controversial meaning and suggested that other vocabulary might be more appropriate.

Certainly, language was a major hurdle as we tried to decide whether or not to use a law whose very name invited controversy. We preferred the vocabulary used by truth commissions, and in our decision to file a lawsuit we agreed to adjust the use of language as much as possible. Thus in drafting a press release to coincide with the filing of our complaint, we tried to minimize use of the word "terrorism," substituting it with "assassination," which carried the more specific meaning of "politically motivated murder."

Truth commissions operate on the premise that it is the individual who has the power to continue or break cycles of violence. In working to help defeat cycles of violence, they strive to identify and meet the most essential needs of victims. It is those needs—public recognition of wrong-doing, acceptance of responsibility, and expression of remorse by the perpetrator; in short, a full declaration of the truth—that give the commissions their name. Andrew listed all of these criteria when he expressed his vision of justice in Dad's name.

It was perhaps surprising that Andrew and my mother should both cite the work of truth commissions in their visions of ideal justice, because in many ways they represented polar opposite views within our family group. While Andrew was convinced that, ultimately, Dad's assassins should be brought to justice and punished for their crimes, my mother's desire was to narrow the gap in understanding that existed between our society and that of the presumed assassin, and to establish some sort of common ground. Ever since Dad's death she had lived according to that goal, by working in the field of education. After teaching for many years at the American University in Cairo, she became coordinator of the Fulbright program in southern California, a government-funded academic exchange program that brought visiting scholars from around the world to American universities and sent American scholars to study abroad. Where justice for Dad was concerned, she was interested more in rehabilitation and reconciliation than she was in formal courtroom justice and punishment, which she perceived as adversarial. She did not want to widen gaps of understanding.

However, the truth commissions, about which my mother spoke wistfully, did not aim to replace traditional justice, but rather to set down a foundation upon which justice could be built. That foundation would consist of a body of interviews with victims, and sometimes perpetrators,

Visiting my mother, Ann, in Cairo, 1988, at the Muhammad Ali Mosque.

which was unburdening for victims and which allowed perpetrators to acknowledge responsibility for their actions. In some countries such interviews numbered in the tens of thousands and served to establish a public record of wrongdoing—of the truth.

In Argentina and Chile, those bodies of evidence eventually contributed to courtroom justice. Argentinean courts prosecuted nine of the most senior military junta leaders of the previous regime on the basis of information drawn from interviews by the National Commission on the Disappeared.[18] Similarly in 2002, the Spanish judge Baltasar Gazon drew heavily on the work of the Chilean truth commission in building his case for the extradition of General Augusto Pinochet from Britain in order to face charges on the disappearance of Spanish citizens in Chile during the years of his dictatorial rule.[19]

Various truth commissions experimented with this basic structure. South Africa's Truth and Reconciliation Commission, operating in 1996–2000, offered amnesty to perpetrators who gave full accounts of their actions. However, this provision was bitterly contested by some victims, who disputed the right of the commission to offer amnesty. Victims also resented the absence of any requirement for the expression of remorse in exchange for amnesty. Some years later, in 2002, the Commission for Reception, Truth, and Reconciliation for East Timor, taking into account the successes and failures of its predecessors, presented a model similar to the South African one but which instead of amnesty offered the perpetrator the option of community service in lieu of a prison sentence, in exchange for a full acknowledgment of the truth.[20]

The goal in East Timor was twofold: to rehabilitate both the perpetrator and victim. If the scale was small, the essence of the East Timor experiment was pioneering for it addressed both the cause and the consequence of political violence, focusing all the while on the welfare of the individual human being who constitutes the fundamental strand in the fabric of society.

By bringing perpetrator and victim together, truth commissions have succeeded in addressing some of the essential needs of victims. These are needs that the American Antiterrorism Act, in spite of its vast financial resources, cannot. For us there would be no meeting with the perpetrator and no acceptance of responsibility. Furthermore, under the default status that was to arise in every Iran-related case, there would be no defense team present in the courtroom and thus no scrutiny of evidence on the level that we ourselves desired.

Just as South African or East Timorese victims of political violence had to choose whether or not to participate in a framework for justice that had obvious limitations—the absence of a requirement for expression of remorse, or badly needed compensation—so American victims of political violence had to choose whether or not to pursue justice under the terms of a legal framework that had its own imperfections.[21]

■   ■   ■

What I found so difficult to express to Terry Waite was that our decision to initiate a lawsuit was a moral one set against a backdrop of complex international politics. It was motivated by a sense of idealism but tempered, because of those political complexities, by the knowledge that only a limited justice would be possible. I couldn't help thinking that just as Dad had been killed by political crossfire, so we were seeking justice in the very same setting.

I'm sure that Terry would have understood this explanation, just as I'm sure he would have appreciated the addendum that family dynamics as we struggled with our years-long decision making seemed at times almost more complicated than the international politics we were trying so hard to grasp.

What I do remember blurting out instead was, "My brother really wanted to do it." This was a feeble attempt to avoid the bigger, messier picture, and to absolve myself of any misgivings I might have had about our decision. Still, it pointed accurately to Andrew as the catalyst in the formation of that consensus decision. It pointed also to the basic sense of solidarity we all felt in our pursuit, which worked to override our many differences of opinion.

The driving force behind Andrew's wish to initiate a lawsuit was the conviction that to do nothing—to remain passive—carried with it a form of moral guilt. Rama Mani, in a study of the truth commissions entitled *Beyond Retribution,* cites exactly this form of moral guilt as one of the chief obstacles in the path of rebuilding the lives of survivors in the aftermath of political violence.[22] Yet when the Antiterrorism Act was passed in 1996, Andrew recognized at once the instinctive rejection of the rest of us of the whole idea of legal action. He put his loyalty to our mother, John, Steve, and me ahead of his own wishes, casting aside any hopes for legal justice. Of course this meant a terrible conflict, for he was thus unable to carry out the responsibility he felt toward his dead father.

For the next five years, none of us mentioned the subject of a lawsuit. However, all of us were aware that increasing numbers of American families who had been caught in that web of Iranian-sponsored anti-Western violence in Lebanon had decided to take their cases to court. Among these were Tom Sutherland and his family. A Scottish-born agriculturalist, Tom had been Terry Waite's cellmate until the two were released together on November 18, 1991.

Dad had recruited Tom from Colorado State as AUB's dean of agriculture in 1983, and after Dad's assassination Tom had vowed to stay on in

Beirut, determined to uphold the sense of mission that Dad had inspired. Eighteen months later Hizballah kidnapped him. Tom would be one of the longest-held hostages and during his incarceration would often plunge into suicidal depression. Rumors that Tom had tried to kill himself were confirmed after his release, when he described the experience of putting a plastic bag over his head and nearly losing consciousness but prevented from going all the way by images of his wife and daughters. During those long years, I always felt a terrible sense of guilt that Tom's family had to endure such unending agony. When at last he was released, the tables were cruelly turned and Tom and his wife, Jean, took on that same burden of guilt on my mother's behalf.

In the spring of 2001, having recently completed his lawsuit, Tom called my mother in Los Angeles. He and his family had found the legal process, and especially the act of testifying, hugely beneficial. Ten years had passed since his release, but the trial had enabled the family to come together in a way that had not been possible until then.

Moreover, Tom liked and trusted his lawyers, Mike Martinez and Stuart Newberger. He was impressed by their professionalism and compassion and had felt mentored through the legal process. No doubt he wanted my mother to benefit from the same experience. He urged her at least to meet with his lawyers, and somehow that prompted her to suggest to my brothers and me that, at last, we sit down and discuss the possibility of legal action. Even though she herself was still highly reluctant to engage in a lawsuit, she believed it was something that deserved serious family consideration.

Although each of us in our own way had done our best to come to terms with Dad's assassination, that did not necessarily mean that we had fully resolved our feelings of fear and intimidation, anger, guilt, or injustice. Within our family group, all of those emotions were still alive. We were uncomfortable with the murky and complex politics of our case, and we were also quite simply afraid to provoke the perpetrators of the ruthless violence of which Dad had been a target. We argued and discussed for six months on an almost daily basis, relying on e-mail as a way of keeping everyone abreast of every conversation. This exchange culminated in a telephone conference call, during which I heard Andrew cry for the very first time.

With Andrew, Steve, Ann, and John, at home in California, August 2004.

Although we did not see eye to eye on the myriad ethical and political issues bound up in a prospective lawsuit, a visceral bond meant
that there were no constraints upon our willingness to challenge one
another's perceptions, or in our determination to find common ground.
The same sense of family solidarity that had prevented Andrew from
pursuing legal action on his own now shifted position. The rest of us now
understood the depth of Andrew's convictions, and that was perhaps the
most compelling factor propelling us together into consensus building.
Andrew could not bear his sense of failure in doing nothing for Dad, and
we all wanted to find a way of supporting him.

Steve, nonconfrontational by nature and previously not inclined to
initiate a lawsuit, was now firmly committed to going through the process as Andrew's brother. He declared, too, that the moral passivity that
bothered Andrew so much was something he understood and wished to
do something about.

If family duty was at the heart of our decision to go forward, the
other sense of duty that began to grow alongside it was a civic one. Andrew himself insisted during that conference call that he felt a sense of

social responsibility to pursue justice. For me, too, after years of quietly nursing my wounds, a conviction grew up about upholding the rule of law—something without which society unravels. This conviction meant participating fully in a judicial process that I had always taken for granted but now realized embodied both privilege and responsibility. That meant working to help shape and steer the implementation of the Antiterrorism Act, which Stuart Newberger aptly referred to as a work in progress.

As the work of the truth commissions continued to make so clear, ultimately only individual human beings have the power to end cycles of violence. While previously I had assumed that this meant choosing against violent retribution, now I saw that equally, it meant choosing to uphold the rule of law in its capacity as the protector of human rights. Over time, the right of the individual to play a role in the political process became to me an awesome one.

It is one thing to summarize these convictions long after gradually discovering them. At the time of our decision making, all of us felt as if we were walking through a minefield. When at last we agreed to sign the complaint that would put a lawsuit into motion, any sense of achievement eluded us. We were bruised by the hard work of finding common ground, and yet we knew this was only the beginning. Many issues, such as whether or not to include punitive damages in our suit, lay waiting on our table. Further, we knew that the consequences of this first step were not altogether predictable.

That our decision to take this step was made thirty-six hours before the September 11 attacks on Washington and New York was a cruel coincidence. Those events would cause a resurfacing of every doubt, dividing us before we were able to climb back together into a fragile circle of consensus.

5

Knock, and the Door
Shall Be Opened

WHERE WERE YOU WHEN the first and second planes hit the World Trade Center?

I was sitting in the September sunshine at home in England, talking on the telephone with John in Michigan about the virtues of punitive damages. We bantered back and forth for a good half hour, still struggling to understand the practicalities and ethics of this awesome legal device, but enjoying too a newfound sense of relief now that our family had at last come to agreement on filing a lawsuit.

As we talked, our new lawyer at Crowell and Moring, Mike Martinez, sat at his desk in Washington preparing two versions of the legal complaint that all of us would need to sign to put the suit into motion— one version including punitive damages and one not. We hoped to decide on the matter within the next few days and to return the version agreed upon, so that Mike could file our suit in advance of some technical deadline that I didn't understand. Just as John and I were oblivious to unfolding disaster, so Mike did not hear the crash of the third plane some three miles away from his office, a plane that happened to carry a close Martinez family friend.

My son Willem and I spent the next hour happily picking apples from our neighbor's bulging tree and then drove to school to collect his older brothers. That was where the news was broken to me, the only American in the playground. Someone I hardly knew marched up and made the announcement, delivered as a first-rate piece of gossip. Then she marched off again to find her children, leaving me speechless.

I sought out a close friend and began to panic. "What if they come after us again?!" I pictured our address posted on the Internet and Hizballah gunmen moving into East Anglia. Only a tiny part of my consciousness saw the ridiculousness of these wild speculations. My boys and I drove home with the radio blaring news of a fourth plane crash somewhere in Pennsylvania, and with me screaming hysterically for the first time since January 18, 1984, when my mother had telephoned with the news that my father had been shot.

Like many other Americans in the world, I picked up the phone and began to establish contact with my family. None of them was on the East Coast, and of course they were all safe. But each of us felt the same sickening, intimate knowledge of what the families of those killed now faced. Though we had lost no one, the sense of trauma and unreality was uncannily like that which I remembered from all those years before. On the second day, an e-mail came from Mike to say that because of the grounding of air traffic, no mail was going out. The two versions of the complaint had been prepared while the planes had crashed, but they sat in the Crowell and Moring mailbag, waiting even to leave the building. An uneasy feeling welled up inside me as I realized that now we had a little extra time to decide which version to sign.

On the third day, phoning one another yet again, I carelessly mentioned this fact to my mother. Although her reaction provoked new tears, I was not surprised at her angry incredulity that the subject be even remotely discussable under the circumstances.

Andrew, on the other hand, knew exactly which version of the complaint he wanted to sign—though he was ready to sign either one in order to get the process started immediately. In fact, he was now resolved to go forward alone if that's the way it had to be.

. . .

In the days following, we all watched quietly as public reaction took shape. A plumber on a call-out to repair a leak in our bathroom thundered, "We want you to know, we're with you! This is war!" Who was the enemy? Newspapers speculated as to who the culprits might be, and after initial reports of possible Middle Eastern extremists, some dared to suggest that perhaps, as with the Oklahoma City bombing, the answer lay not outside but within American society—though the suggestion was short-lived.

On the Internet, Imad Mughniyeh's name popped up alongside Usama Bin Laden's. Once a Shi'ite boy who grew up alongside the Beirut Airport runway, now Imad Mughniyeh was believed by some to possess a new plastic surgeon's face and was described by one writer as possibly "the world's leading terrorist mastermind."[1] Whether or not the mastermind of September 11, certainly Mughniyeh symbolized the new-age transnational terrorist who had suddenly come to prominence.

Speculation soon turned to anticipation. CNN reporters were posted to Afghanistan, where Usama Bin Laden's people were reportedly hiding out, in anticipation of possible punitive strikes on possible culprits. On the news, I heard Tony Blair pledge his support for George Bush's promise to "hunt down those responsible."

No matter how many times I heard this expression, it always shocked me. How could the world's most powerful politicians believe, or pretend, that the problem they faced had to do with the intentions of specific individuals, rather than with a deep-seated set of values and perceptions pitting whole cultures against one another? It was like promising to "hunt down anger" and eradicate it once and for all!

While the world waited nervously to see what America would do, a gulf between light-skinned Westerners and dark-skinned Easterners widened daily. My mother, in her work as coordinator for the Fulbright program in Southern California, greeted a newly arrived Yemeni professor by the name of Muhammad. With his name, together with his beard and dark skin, she feared the unwelcome reception he might encounter while house hunting. So she decided to put him up in her own guest room. When strangers asked where he was from, he took to answering, "I'm from Fiji!" In Britain, a young Muslim stand-up comic tried to bridge the widening gulf. Dressed in her conservative Muslim attire, she poked fun at "Usama Bin Liner," and made it, temporarily, into all the papers.

Meanwhile, the two versions of the complaint finally reached our mailboxes. But tensions were far too great for us to have any sort of reasonable discussion about what to do. For my mother, a lawsuit was now possibly out of the question. It could, potentially, invite dangerous misinterpretations of adversarial posturing in a time of huge mistrust. Andrew was resolute that now more than ever was the time to take legal action. John was impatient to move on and to get this chapter of his life over with. I felt caught between them and felt no clear sense of direction.

Then out of the blue, an Arab-American friend in Texas e-mailed me exultantly to say that Steve, now a favorite NBA player on the San Antonio Spurs basketball team, had taken his family to dine at a shunned Arab restaurant in town. The response had been overwhelming, and the restaurant had come back to life.

Characteristically soft-spoken inside our family circle, Steve had said nothing about the lawsuit since September 11. But his actions spoke volumes. A day or two later, finding himself on a local radio show, he took further advantage of his natural platform and asked his listeners if they would reject the characterization of all Americans as "Timothy McVeigh," in a challenge to those tempted to characterize all Arabs as terrorists.

Perhaps it was Steve's unplanned public stance that gave my mother and me the courage to proceed with our own action against political violence in the form of a lawsuit. There was, too, the instinctive concern that now more than ever, this was something none of us should do alone. We agreed to sign the version of the complaint that did not include punitive damages because we understood that we could always add punitives at a later date—though the reverse would not be possible. We drafted a press statement that carefully reflected our intentions of going into the process with an open mind. On September 20, Mike e-mailed us all to say that our case had that day been filed in the U.S. District Court for the District of Columbia and assigned to Judge Thomas Penfold Jackson.

While at first September 11 threatened to undermine the very viability of a lawsuit under the Antiterrorism Act, ultimately it served to define our approach to it. Legislation enabling the indefinite detention of suspected "terrorists," huge confusion in the public mind about the Arab and Islamic worlds, and widespread support for the use of force against suspected culprits, drove home the imperative need for a careful, informed, and above all peaceful approach to the kind of political violence that long ago had shattered our lives and now engulfed the American psyche.

. . .

From a legal standpoint, the purpose of the trial was to satisfy the terms of the law: to convince the judge that the Iranian government was responsible for Dad's assassination through its direct political and financial patronage of Hizballah, and the specific policy of eliminating a series of American targets. Evidence would be drawn from declassified U.S. intelligence documents retrieved under the Freedom of Information Act and then supplemented by the testimony of two or three key expert witnesses who understood the context in which those documents had been prepared and could extrapolate on their wider meaning.

To us, the requirements of the law seemed narrow and the means of satisfying its terms parochial. We wanted personally to be convinced of the case put before the court in the very broadest sense, which we knew would mean going beyond the traditional scope of inquiry. We wanted to understand, too, why Dad, an Arabist and Islamicist eulogized by Arabs and Muslims for his committed but critical stance, made sense as a target of Iran's Islamic revolution. If others accepted this, it was nevertheless something we found hard to believe.

But adequate evidence already existed, our lawyers believed, to win the case. Indeed they would not have taken us on as clients had they not believed it was true. Neither would the U.S. District Court, one presided over by a dozen presidentially appointed district judges, have allowed the filing of a complaint without confidence in its base of evidence.

This evidence consisted mainly of a collection of declassified intelligence documents unearthed in research for previous Hizballah-related casework and was shown to us at our preliminary meeting at Crowell and Moring's London office. None of it was precise raw data pertaining primarily to Dad. Rather, it contained serious reference to Dad as a victim of Hizballah, apparently on the basis of the sort of raw intelligence that Andrew had seen during his days at the National Security Council.

Several documents stood out among the rest: in particular, a series of CIA Directorate of Operations memos generated in conjunction with the

March 16, 1984, kidnapping of the CIA's William Buckley. The first memo was dated April 4, 1984, with the subject heading "Islamic Jihad Claims Responsibility for Buckley Kidnapping."[2] It referred to an event three hours and fifteen minutes before when "[BLANK] found an envelope pushed under his door. In the envelope were a slip of paper and another sealed envelope. The slip of paper contained instructions, printed in perfect English, telling [BLANK] to follow instructions exactly, not to open the second envelope and to deliver the envelope by hand to the American Ambassador." All this took place at the American Embassy in Algiers.

Inside the second envelope were five Polaroid photos of the recent Hizballah-held kidnap victims: besides Buckley, there were CNN Beirut bureau chief Jeremy Levin, AUB professor Frank Regier, a Frenchman by the name of Christian Joubert, and the Saudi Arabian consul Husayn Abdallah Farrash. The photos of the Americans were all taken in the same room, although as later became known, Regier was held together only with the Frenchman and never saw Buckley or Levin during his incarceration. An accompanying slip of paper was signed by "Islamic Jihad." (Later that month Regier and Joubert were removed from the equation when, in their makeshift South Beirut prison, they were spotted by a group of children and allowed to escape.)[3]

A second memo in the series, entitled "Buckley Kidnapping Talking Points," concluded that Buckley's kidnapping was not an isolated event but part of a concerted campaign aimed at eliminating American and Western influence in Lebanon.[4] This campaign had so far included such events as the April 1983 bombing of the U.S. Embassy, the October 1983 bombing of the American marine and French barracks, the January 1984 assassination of AUB president Malcolm Kerr, and the kidnappings of those mentioned in the first memo, along with a new hostage, Presbyterian minister Ben Weir, who was snatched in May.

A third memo in the series, dated June 25, 1984, and entitled "Buckley Kidnapping Update" stated that earlier that same day, "[BLANK] informed the American Ambassador in [BLANK] that Hizballah was indeed holding Buckley, Levin and Weir, in addition to Saudi Consul Farrash. Further, Hizballah was willing to release the kidnap victims provided that [BLANK] informed Ambassador Newlin that Hizballah was supported by Iran and in particular by Iranian Foreign Minister Velyati." A final paragraph stated, "It has long been rumored that Hizballah wished to trade the kidnappees for the detainees in Kuwait, but this appears to be the first Hizballah attempt to enter into negotiations in this regard."[5]

There were two crucial aspects to these memos. One, as Andrew concurred, was their high level of reliability owing to their select circulation. They had been prepared exclusively for the daily meeting between the CIA director and the president at the president's briefing on security issues. Such briefings would be based not on speculation, but on explicit information acquired from intelligence sources such as wiretaps, satellite images, and so forth. Such sources were obvious in the first and third memos. In the second memo one had to assume that the allegation regarding Dad was made on the basis of similarly direct sources.

The other crucial aspect of the memos was the linkage of events that established a compelling picture of an anti-Western campaign. I could not fully appreciate the significance of these linkages when I first laid eyes on the memos. But over the fifteen months leading up to our trial, as the story fleshed out from a broad range of sources, that significance became overwhelmingly convincing to me. Looking at these linkages in chronological order, the skeleton framework is established: the responsibility for the kidnapping of the Saudi consul, who was seized on the day before Dad was killed, was officially announced in the same statement which claimed responsibility for Dad's assassination, made by telephone to Agence France-Presse a few hours after Dad's body was brought to the AUB hospital.

Less than a month later, Frank Regier was kidnapped, and though he never saw or met the Saudi consul, Buckley, or Levin during his nine weeks of captivity, these captives were linked by virtue of their photographs being taken in the same room and delivered together in that envelope directed to the American ambassador in Algiers. They were linked further when Levin, following his escape, was able to describe to U.S. intelligence officials the location of his place of incarceration in the Bekaa Valley. U.S. intelligence in turn identified that location to be the Lebanese National Army barracks in Baalbek but seized in the summer of 1982 by the Iranian Revolutionary Guard. The barracks had become Hizballah headquarters.[6]

In this circuitous fashion, Dad was linked to the Saudi consul, who was linked to Levin, who was linked to Hizballah.

Evidence that these linked events constituted part of an anti-Western campaign strengthened as time went on. For example, in September 1984 the new U.S. Embassy building in Beirut, which replaced the one blown up in April 1983, was itself blown up by a truck bomb. U.S. satellite intelligence photos captured a mock-up of the new embassy at Hizballah headquarters in the Bekaa Valley.[7]

As for Buckley, he was later held captive alongside Weir, whose release eventually was achieved through the arms-for-hostages deal, when American Hawk missiles were delivered to Iran in a secret agreement between the Reagan administration and the Iranian government.

This was the basic structure upon which our legal case would be built.

■   ■   ■

Although at that first meeting in London I was interested in the CIA memos, there were no raw data focusing on Dad. Andrew had had his moment of overwhelming revelation during his time at the NSC, but the rest of us had not. Although we believed in the existence and credibility of the damning evidence Andrew had seen, and indeed probably would not have embarked on a lawsuit without knowledge of it, still it mattered enormously that every one of us see direct, compelling evidence with our own eyes. But Andrew felt sure that his smoking gun was unlikely to be released under the Freedom of Information Act, perhaps because of the manner in which it had been obtained. Therefore our case would have to do without it.

With or without it, there was a further unsettling feeling that this traditional line of inquiry was confined to government intelligence sources and took inadequate notice of the expertise of international academia, journalism, and other regional-based expertise. Even the memoir of Robert Baer, the ex–CIA Beirut station chief, was damningly critical of the ability of the CIA to acquire a decent standard of intelligence because it had failed to produce a new generation of agents trained in language and culture. Too often, Baer chastised, spying was carried out from desks in Washington.

We had grown up in a world in which academics and journalists lived in the places they studied, giving them an empathetic understanding of the people who lived there. In the post–September 11 atmosphere of quick judgments and conclusions, that kind of intimate knowledge and human familiarity was dangerously absent.

We were concerned, too, because of the inevitable default status of our case, which meant there would be no defense team to represent the Iranian government and to challenge the evidence presented on our behalf. This reinforced our inclination to challenge and question, and to support evidence we trusted through scrutiny of other sources.

Our lawyers understood our position from the start. They accepted, too, that although we considered this an important legal exercise promoting nonviolent response to a deadly deed, it was also a unique opportunity for us to learn as much as we could about what had happened to Dad in a way we would never again undertake.

. . .

For all our wishes and intentions to study and learn, by the time the complaint was filed we were drained and exhausted, and let the matter rest for a time. It was a blessing that the machinations of the legal system provided a hiatus and the chance for us to gather our wits.

The complaint was translated into Farsi and then handed to a Swiss envoy in Geneva, who would deliver it personally to the Ministry of Information and Security in Tehran. For the moment, there was nothing for us to do but wait as our lawyers began to tackle the case.

This period of respite would last for several months, taking into account the legally requisite period of sixty days that the defendant was given to make a formal response. It would be well into spring when, with no response from the Iranian side, Judge Jackson entered a default status on *Kerr v. Islamic Republic of Iran*. We understood that the Iranian position was not a rejection of the accusation contained in the claim, but rather a rejection of the jurisdiction of U.S. courts to try the case.

Nevertheless, our lawyers began their work of gathering evidence as soon as we signed the complaint. In fact, as Tom Sutherland had suggested months before, Crowell and Moring, rapidly assuming pre-eminence as legal counsel to a large number of Hizballah's American victims, would probably research Dad's case regardless of whether we decided to file a suit. They needed to be confident in their expertise on Dad's position in the scheme of things in order to best serve the other cases on their table.

Thus, a full-fledged Freedom of Information Act search on Malcolm Kerr was initiated. The lumbering process of bureaucracy meant that it could take months, even years, to retrieve copies of all the documents mentioning Dad's name which were filed away in various government agencies and departments—the National Security Agency, the State Department, the CIA, the Reagan Library, and other locations.

During this initial phase, a few documents began to trickle back to us. For months they contained little or nothing new, but they did provide a beginner's lesson on the Freedom of Information Act. The words "Freedom of Information" seemed hardly apt, for a black marking pen was applied liberally by whoever was in charge of putting U.S. intelligence into the public domain. Essential names, dates, and other data were quite literally blacked out, often rendering a document practically useless. Sometimes, computerized cutting of large amounts of text would result in blank page after blank page. I counted thirty-eight blank pages in one document and marveled at the effort of getting them to me: the request, the retrieval, the photocopying, and the mailing of fresh scrap paper for my children.

A rare example of completely uncensored documentation was a citizen's letter of concern written by my cousin Nancy Jessup in the wake of the American bombing of Libya in April 1986—the same event that had precipitated the sale and execution of three Hizballah hostages. Nancy's letter identified herself as Malcolm Kerr's niece and the letter was given status requiring "reply within nine days." A response on President Reagan's behalf, expressing sympathy for Nancy's concern but reiterating American policy, was drafted by the appropriate clerk.[8] The correspondence was released to us in its entirety—no black marking pens here.

The lack of any new or significant information increased my mother's skepticism about the strength of evidence to be put before the court. She wrote to Mike Martinez, expressing her doubts and asking again whether any possibility existed for a subpoena of what we now called "Andrew's document"—without which our documentary evidence looked worryingly secondhand. The advice was to wait and see what transpired.

In March 2002, six months after the filing of our complaint, Mike wrote to us all to sum up where things seemed to be going. The CIA, it seemed, was not cooperating with our FOIA requests. They had written to Crowell and Moring to say that their search was done and that they had found only two documents to release. But Crowell and Moring knew that other documents ought to have been released because they had already surfaced in conjunction with other cases. The lawyers pointed that out to the CIA and added that the CIA had not even released partially redacted documents, as they were required to do.

This state of affairs was sobering to say the least. Our government had passed the Antiterrorism Act, which encouraged us to seek justice through a civil lawsuit, but then made it difficult to obtain the information required to do a proper job.

Frustration eroded our trust in whatever information we were allowed to see. At times some of us wondered what it was we were not being told. Two lines in a thirteen-page document generated the day after Dad was killed referred to his assassination, but the rest of the document consisted of blank white pages. Was there some other, horrible dimension to the story?

There was another weakness, which was the appearance of occasional inaccuracies. In October 2002 we received a document originating from the Foreign Broadcast Service, dated October 1995 and entitled, "American University Produces Nationalists." It contained a brief sketch of Dad's career, misquoting the titles of his books and giving the wrong year for the date of his assassination. Although it was a piece of journalism and not the product of U.S. intelligence, still it planted a warning about the reliability of sources generally, and indeed our ability to judge the accuracy of information coming our way.

The time had come to begin in earnest our own quest to understand what had happened to Dad by looking outside the domain of government intelligence. My mother tapped her wide network of Middle East–based friends and associates, while I began to read.

.   .   .

I was drawn first back to Terry Anderson's memoir, in part, I suppose, because I was seeking a commonality of experience that would provide some kind of comfort. But of course, too, the book contained that very first suggestion that Iran and Hizballah had been responsible for Dad's murder: that infamous footnote that described the issuing of a fatwa as "a religious ruling—issued by Hizballah's ruling council, condemning Kerr to death."[9] I knew from the document Andrew had seen that, essentially, this was a good place to begin.

The notion of this fatwa, and the idea that we might find some record of it, had obsessed me since our initial meeting with the lawyers in London, when we had had our first look at evidence and discussed how we might proceed. The fatwa seemed pivotal because it would have been a formal directive issued from a position of authority. It was now widely believed that Hizballah's ruling council of the day had had inextricable links with senior Iranian government representatives. It pointed to the state sponsorship of terrorism that our lawsuit was all about.

While I had many misgivings about my own government's sins in enlarging the problems of Lebanon—whether through ineptitude or cowardice or selfish ambition—and while I felt sure that the carrying out of Dad's assassination probably included, indirectly, individuals from outside the Hizballah umbrella, I was absolutely resolved to take a stance against any form of violence as official government policy. I wanted to see with my own eyes a record of that policy.

Would the fatwa have been published in a newspaper? Where was the paper trail? I knew little about this subject. For me as for other ordinary people, the term "fatwa" had been sensationalized by media coverage of high-profile cases like that of the British author Salman Rushdie, following the publication of his book *The Satanic Verses*. Rushdie had spent years in hiding, protected by British police at huge expense to taxpayers.

I telephoned Terry Anderson to inquire further about his footnote, and a path of investigation opened up for me. He explained the Shi'ite relationship of mentor and disciple, in which authority must be sought and granted before the carrying out of a particular deed. Traditionally, the mentor is a clerical leader (imam), and authority is granted in an oral manner. In this command structure and its particular manifestation in January 1984, a possible scenario might have been that the Hizballah organization recognized Malcolm Kerr as a suitable target in its anti-Western campaign, and that authority would have been sought from the top of the chain of command. A ruling would have been issued condemning him to death but leaving the carrying out of the deed to local hit men—either hired or from within the Hizballah group. Throughout the chain of command, authority and instructions would have been issued orally.

The point was that there would be no paper trail, and that the key to understanding the fatwa was to understand the Shi'ite culture of authority. That meant moving completely outside of my own culture and understandings of decision making. Anderson recommended reading the works of academics, as he had done. While I had read a little about Shi'ism in my university days, I'd hardly opened a book on the subject since Dad was killed. A whole body of literature had emerged in the intervening years, shedding light on the radicalization of Shi'ism during that critical time.

In particular, he suggested the work of Nikki Keddie, who as Dad's UCLA colleague I remembered from childhood Christmas parties and faculty gatherings. In fact I recalled having one of her books somewhere on my shelves and found it now: it was *Shi'ism and Social Protest,* edited with Juan Cole. When I opened it I discovered why she had given us this volume, for it was dedicated to Dad: "Malcolm Kerr, Scholar, Teacher, Friend, Partisan of Peace and Justice in the Middle East . . . extraordinary human being, whose contribution to the understanding of the Middle East was probably unparalleled in his generation." It went on, "Our dedication of this volume to him reflects no opinion regarding the still-unresolved question of who his killer was."[10]

While this caveat reflected the bewildering chaos of Lebanon and the mystery of Dad's assassins in 1986, the year the book was published, now it provided much of the essential background to understanding how it was that he had been in the wrong place at the wrong time.

.　.　.

The Shi'a branch of Islam grew out of a dispute in the early Muslim community over succession to the leadership of the prophet Muhammad. One group favored hereditary succession of the descendants of Muhammad through his son-in-law, Ali; this group became known as the party of Ali, or *Shi'iat 'Ali,* now Anglicized as "Shi'ites." The other group, the Sunnis, favored elected leadership.

In the year 680, the two sides met in battle at Karbala in present-day Iraq—a target of U.S. fighter planes in 2003. There, Ali's son Husayn was mortally wounded, and the Shi'ite movement was born out of the loss and martyrdom of its leader. The Sunnis emerged the victors.

The theology that emerged out of the Shi'ite movement differed from that of mainstream, orthodox Sunni Islam in its expectation of a messianic leader, or *mahdi,* who would restore justice after a period of injustice and oppression.

Over time, the Sunnis would dominate politically in a vast and prosperous empire that for hundreds of years stretched from Spain across North Africa into the Middle East and central, south, and southeast Asia. This was hardly a religion confined to the Arab world, although its language, that of the Qur'an, was Arabic. This Islamic empire would produce the greatest scientists of their age, as well as historians, artists, and architects, at a time when Europe was mired in the Dark Ages.

In its minority position, and growing as it did out of the death of its leader, Husayn, martyrdom and victimization were among the defining characteristics of Shi'ite culture. Emotional commemoration of Husayn's martyrdom in passion plays marked the annual rites of *Ashura.* At times, secrecy would be an important resource for survival and continuity. Shi'ite communities dotted across regions now known as Lebanon, Iraq, Iran, Afghanistan, Pakistan, and India were marked by fierce loyalty and self-reliance.

These communities were led by local imams, or clerics. For hundreds of years, young men from far and wide traveled back to the place of

Husayn's martyrdom, Karbala; to Najaf (also in present-day Iraq and another target of the 2003 U.S. military machine); and to Qom, in present-day Iran. In those cities they were taught in the *madrasa*s, or schools, according to traditional principles and methods and in which the Qur'an was the basic text.

Teachers in these religious schools were by definition imams, and the key characteristic in the relationship between teacher and student was that of mentor and disciple. In the absence of political power in the wider, ruling state, the clerical mentor's authority within the Shi'ite community was critical.

It was out of this tradition that in the late 1970s the Western-oriented and secular leadership of Iran's shah was challenged by the clerical leadership of Iran's Shi'ite community. The base of support for this clerical leadership was huge because of the modern-day Shi'ite strength in Iran. Many factors contributed to a time ripe for the Islamic revolution. The shah's courting of what was seen as an imperialist West, his ruthless police state with its sophisticated intelligence network, and the growth of secular nationalist ideologies in neighboring Arab countries inspired clerics like the Ayatollah Khomeini to lecture in the late 1960s and 1970s in the holy city of Najaf on revolutionary Islamic doctrine and visions of a new Islamic state.

In 1979 Khomeini and his following succeeded in deposing the shah. Reza Pahlavi, as he was by then known, took refuge in Cairo. The Islamic revolution gripped Iran, and one of its early acts of breathtaking audacity was the seizure of fifty-four U.S. Embassy staff members in Tehran, and their captivity for 444 days. Even visually the country transformed from a Western-oriented society to one in which Islamic dress symbolized a complete change in attitude. These outward symbols captured the imagination of the outside world, and the embassy hostage crisis demonstrated the effectiveness of using random humans for political manipulation. Jimmy Carter's presidency fell spectacularly on its inability to resolve the crisis.

In the summer of 1980, Reza Pahlavi, the former shah, died in Egypt. The occasion inspired an Iranian radio station to announce, "The bloodsucker of the century is dead at last." Out of curiosity and living in Cairo at the time, I made my way to the shah's funeral procession on an oven-hot day. The streets were packed, and thousands more watched from windows, though the mood was one of subdued curiosity more than anything. I saw Richard Nixon and Anwar Sadat, the Egyptian president, march behind the coffin, symbolizing the imperialist and the secular nationalist so despised by the new Iran.

But apart from Sadat, there were no Arab leaders present. A few years earlier Sadat had isolated Egypt, once the leader of pan-Arab nationalism, by his recognition of Israel. The fact that the shah had taken refuge in the only Arab country that shared an open border with Israel added to the humiliation of his exile and fanned fires in Iran.

A year later Sadat would be assassinated by soldiers loyal to the Muslim Brotherhood, shot in a grandstand while he was watching a military parade. He was succeeded by his vice president, Hosni Mubarak, who survived the attack and would rule with an increasingly iron fist. Around that time Dad was teaching at the American University in Cairo, where the former shah's son was enrolled in his introductory course on Middle East politics (prompting much mirth around the dinner table). Dad often speculated as to whether Egypt would turn into another Iran, whose revolution he characterized in 1981 by the prophetic words, "virulent xenophobia and punitive hostility."[11] But such qualities, he always went on to say, did not describe Egypt, a country marked by a disarming openness to outsiders. And the Shi'ite base was not there.

Indeed, the very title of Keddie and Cole's volume, *Shi'ism and Social Protest*, reflects the defining characteristic of this branch of Islam. A Shi'ite movement of social protest in Iraq, the al-Dawa Party, also growing out of the 1970s Najaf and Karbala schools, met the challenge of Saddam Hussein's ruling Baathists. Al-Dawa was forced underground but remained quietly active. Its members were close familial relatives of those Lebanese Shi'ites who would soon become members of the new Hizballah, or Party of God.

Conditions for Shi'ite social protest in Lebanon were different again. Terry Anderson remarked at our trial that Iran's goal of an Islamic revolution in Lebanon, ruthlessly pursued for a nearly a decade, "almost worked." But Lebanon, a tiny but strategically situated country whose modern boundaries emerged from the mapmaking of Western powers at the Paris Peace Conference in the aftermath of World War I, comprised a hugely diverse society of not only Sunni and Shi'ite Muslims but also Maronite, Armenian, and Greek Orthodox Christians; Druze (an offshoot of another sectarian branch of Islam); and, since the establishment of the Israeli state in 1948, a large Palestinian refugee population. That diversity was the source of conflict in Lebanon's civil war, which in turn created the absence of authority that rendered Lebanon so vulnerable to the ambitions of outsiders like Iran, Syria, and Israel. But that diversity was also the variable that, ultimately, the Islamic revolution could not overcome.

Out of that mix of sectarian Lebanese communities, the Shi'ites never held their proportional share of political power. It was primarily the Maronite Christians and to a lesser extent the Sunni Muslims, patronized at different points in history by Christian crusaders, Sunni Ottomans, and then postwar France and Britain, who enjoyed traditional preeminence. This prerogative was reflected in Lebanon's constitution, which reserves the office of president for a Maronite and that of prime minister for a Sunni Muslim. The largely ineffectual position of speaker of the house was allocated to the Shi'ites, who were thus marginalized in the national politics of newly independent Lebanon.

In time, the Shi'ite population of Lebanon burgeoned through its high birth rate and by the 1960s was believed to constitute a far higher proportion of the overall population than was reflected in its allocation of political power. An update of the census of 1932, upon which this allocation was ostensibly based, was carefully avoided. But disquiet over their political disenfranchisement nevertheless grew.

Several events were to have a profound effect upon the evolution of the Shi'ite community and its role in Lebanon. The first was the arrival in the ancient southern coastal city of Tyre in 1962 of a new imam to preside over the Shi'ite community there. He was Musa Sadr, a young Iranian from the town of Qom. Musa Sadr's natural recruitment from Iran symbolized the strong links that connected the Shi'ite clerics of Lebanon, Iraq, and Iran, and their families.

A charismatic man who was quickly embraced by his new community, Musa Sadr galvanized his constituents into the fold of a new movement for social justice. He called it the Movement for the Deprived, and its primary goal was the improvement of the lives of ordinary Shi'ites through education and social welfare. Musa Sadr was called *murshid al-ruhi* or "spiritual guide"—the same term later used to describe Khomeini in Iran. Unlike Khomeini in the Islamic revolution, Musa Sadr did not seek to divorce his community from multifaith Lebanon but rather to give it a voice within the national framework.

In 1975 the movement took on a broader scope when it acquired its own armed militia and became known as Afwaj al-Muqawamah al-Lubnaniyah (Battalions of the Lebanese Resistance), and more commonly according to its acronym, Amal, meaning "hope."

A second event occurred in 1975, when a civil war erupted in Lebanon. Though its long-term causes were many (in particular, the steady growth in the power of the Palestine Liberation Organization, or PLO), it was sparked in April 1975 when a group of Phalangist militiamen—the military wing of the Maronite Christians—massacred a bus full of Palestinians traveling through a Christian neighborhood in Ain Rummaneh. There occurred, too, the challenge of the Druze leader Kamal Jumblatt to Maronite supremacy. Jumblatt's militia, incorporating large numbers of Shi'ites, suffered enormous loss of life but was rescued by Syria. Syria had its own designs on Lebanon, standing as it did between itself and Israel—with which Syria was at war and which had occupied Syria's Golan Heights since the 1967 Arab-Israeli war. With Syria drawn into the fray, the Lebanese civil war was given new lifeblood and new dimensions took shape.

My mother took me to visit Lebanon a year or so into the civil war. On a quiet day we saw the staggering destruction of downtown Beirut by the sheer force of bullets. In the Druze mountain village of Ainab, where my grandparents had built a house in the early 1930s and where I had spent many an idyllic summer, even our own little stone dwelling had been looted and the surrounding woods burned. Ainab's commanding view of Beirut and the coastline was now a liability rather than an asset. Driving back to Beirut I saw a small boy carrying a gun.

A third event concerned the Palestinian refugee presence in Lebanon. Palestinian refugees from all walks of life—doctors, farmers, teachers, and merchants—fled their homes in what had been Palestine when it was violently superseded by the new state of Israel in 1948. The refugee status of tens of thousands of Palestinians was never resolved, and most lived in poverty-stricken shanty camps enduring through generations, adding another element to the already complex mix of coexisting religious, ethnic, and national groups in Lebanon.

The situation was compounded further when in 1970 the PLO was evicted from Jordan in King Hussein's own quest for political survival. Jordan, also created during the mapmaking days of the Paris Peace Conference, had like Lebanon absorbed Palestinian refugee populations in the wake of Arab-Israeli wars. However in Jordan, the Palestinians outnumbered the indigenous population. While the integration of civilian Palestinians into Jordanian society somehow worked, political integration of Palestinian nationalists—who in 1967 organized themselves under the umbrella of the militant PLO—did not.

So the PLO leadership relocated to Beirut, and its fighting power established itself in south Lebanon along the Israeli border—to the chagrin of the Shi'ite community there, who became caught in the crossfire of an endless cycle of retaliatory raids and punitive strikes. Thus the Lebanese civil war took in not only Syrian-Israeli animosity but the core Palestinian-Israeli conflict as well. The United States, which openly financed the dominant Israeli military and refused to join the international community in its condemnation of Israel's many violations of UN Resolutions, was considered a key factor in the equation.

While many Americans may have had a general awareness of their government's support for Israel, what that support meant to those directly concerned in the Middle East—the Israelis who received the support and the Palestinian Arabs who did not—was vividly and passionately understood there. It was perhaps impossible for ordinary Americans living halfway across the world to have realized the resentment among ordinary Arabs toward the U.S. government, but still it was real. And as Israel's American-funded exploits went unchecked by the U.S. government, resentment of Americans by the victims of those exploits grew.

By the late 1970s, the plight of the Lebanese Shi'ite community was dire. Musa Sadr's program of social welfare had been marred by the enlarging civil war. In the south, Shi'ite homes were bulldozed or blown up—a punitive ploy of the Israeli army used regularly against Palestinians but used also against the Shi'ites because the groups lived alongside one another. Many Shi'ites fled to Beirut, particularly in 1978 when the Israeli army moved into the south of Lebanon. But as refugees with no urban base of support, many Shi'ites took up residence in the Palestinian refugee camps of south Beirut.

While initially the Shi'ites had resented Palestinian presence in Lebanon, their anger now turned to the invading Israelis. An alliance of sorts evolved between the Shi'ites and Palestinians, based on common circumstance and a common enemy.

Meanwhile, another alliance formed between Maronite Christians and Israelis, the latter acting as patron to the former. From 1978, a Lebanese Christian army, supplied, trained, and financed by Israel—and by extension, the United States—patrolled the Israeli-controlled south, its soldiers enjoying a monthly stipend, which at the time was the highest offered by any militia.

Animosity between impoverished and politically powerless Palestinians and Shi'ites on the one hand and properly financed and politically dominant Maronites and Israelis on the other was extreme.

In 1978, the year that Israel invaded southern Lebanon, the Shi'ite community lost its spiritual guide when Imam Musa Sadr vanished during a trip to Libya. This event prompted vast speculation and remains unresolved to this day. If he was a charismatic figure before, now Musa Sadr took on cult status. Many Shi'ites interpreted his disappearance according to strict theological doctrine, as an act of occultation, or hiding, which would be followed by the appearance of a *mahdi*, or messianic figure.

Without a doubt, Musa Sadr's disappearance left a spiritual and political vacuum in the Lebanese Shi'ite community. His role as the head of Amal was eventually filled by the unlikely figure of Nabih Berri, who was not only a noncleric but also a Sierra Leone–born, U.S. green-card holder with an ex-wife and children in Dearborn, Michigan. Nevertheless, he took control of political Amal, whose militia had become one of many factors in the fighting that made up the Lebanese civil war.

Berri's Western, secular credentials did not serve him well at a time when the Islamic revolution was about to erupt in Shi'ite Muslim Iran.

Some Shi'ites labeled Berri a Western-oriented hypocrite, and his position at the head of Amal perhaps helped to provoke the conditions for a radical split among the Shi'ites of Lebanon.

By early 1982, the Islamic revolution was well established in Iran and enjoying the fervent confidence of its early days. Unable to establish a footing in Saddam Hussein's Iraq, the revolution looked to Lebanon. With its large and discontented Shi'ite population, its lack of national authority, and an imperialist enemy in the form of Israel and America, Lebanon was ripe for the export of Iran's fundamentalist blueprint for a new Islamic order.

Of course historical trends are most easily observed in hindsight. At the time, rather than the coming of the Islamic revolution, some saw hopeful signs of an end to Lebanon's civil war. Although plans and ideas were developing in Iran, Lebanon itself was relatively quiet in the dawn of 1982.

Dad was one of those who wished to see signs of hope. When the AUB presidency was offered to him in March 1982, he gambled and accepted. But by the time he arrived in Beirut several months later, everything had changed.

On June 6, 1982, the Israeli Army invaded Lebanon, moving quickly all the way to Beirut, and the United States failed to challenge its forward march. We read in the papers of the unfathomable sight of General Ariel Sharon celebrating in an East Beirut bar. Within two weeks of the invasion, on the pretext of joining Lebanon in the fight against Israel, Iran persuaded Syria to allow its Revolutionary Guard into the country by way of the Syrian-controlled Damascus-Beirut Highway. Iran soon established its foothold in the Bekaa Valley and the Hizballah organization was born. Israel's bombing of Beirut carried on for three months and culminated in its occupation of the city and the expulsion of the PLO leadership from Lebanon. Yasser Arafat and his supporters set sail for Tunisia, leaving thousands of Palestinian refugees unprotected in their camps.

A month after the Israeli invasion and weeks after the formation of Hizballah, AUB's vice president, David Dodge, was kidnapped. Magnus Ranstorp, author of *Hizballah in Lebanon*, describes the kidnapping as the first target of the new Hizballah's anti-American campaign.[12] Dodge

Left to right: Najeeb Halaby, AUB board chairman; Senator Charles Percy; Dad; and David Dodge, AUB vice president, in Senator Percy's Washington office discussing AUB's future, late March 1982. Dad was very newly appointed as AUB's president and the Israeli invasion of Lebanon was ten weeks away. David would be kidnapped by Hizballah in July.

himself believed he was taken as an act of protest against an invasion that America had the power to stop.[13]

We guessed that Dad should have been the one taken, but at the time he was waiting out the war at AUB's New York office. His lifelong friend, who had also grown up on the AUB campus, had stepped into the role of acting president.

Dad's arrival in Beirut on August 21 came just after the Dodge kidnapping and just before the assassination of the new Israeli-supported Lebanese Maronite president Bashir Gemayel in a huge car bomb, and then the massacre of eight hundred Palestinians and Shi'ites at the Sabra and Shatila refugee camps by the Israeli-supervised Maronite Phalange militia.

Although the deadly conditions of life in Beirut at the time were obscenely obvious, chaos and confusion overwhelmed any clear understanding of what was going on. Twenty years later, we benefited from research gradually carried out on this complex subject, which was only

beginning to be understood. It was vital to making sense of the declassified intelligence documents that would constitute the basis of documentary evidence in our case. Those documents might have suggested to us
who did what and when, but not why.

.   .   .

Keddie and Cole's study of Shi'ism in contemporary Lebanon was one of
many works that together provided a broad understanding of the events
and circumstances that led to the targeting of Americans in the 1980s.
Other names, those of academics, journalists, and others who had lived in
Lebanon for many years and cared deeply about why things had gone so
badly wrong—not only for Americans but mainly for the Lebanese whose
country this was—became familiar to me. Among them were Robert Fisk,
the *Independent* correspondent and British author famous for his scathing
condemnation of American policy in the Middle East; Thomas Friedman,
another author and journalist writing for the *New York Times;* Helena Cob-
ban, an expert on the Shi'ites of Lebanon writing for the *Christian Science
Monitor;* and Augustus Richard Norton, an academic and former UN ob-
server who drew his intimate knowledge of radical Shi'ite politics from
time spent in Lebanon. There was, too, a whole body of literature written
in English by Arab historians that offered to take the reader deep inside
the Lebanese experience. Because the declassified intelligence memos we
were seeing lacked historical and human detail, this literature added context and meaning.

Friedman's memoir, *From Beirut to Jerusalem,* is a case in point. He describes the insensitivity to local people of an Israeli army unit on patrol in
south Lebanon. On October 16, 1983, in the market town of Nabatiya, an
Israeli military convoy drove directly through a gathering of some 50,000
to 60,000 Shi'ite Muslims who were in the midst of their ritual *Ashura* commemoration of Husayn's martyrdom at Karbala. The rituals were intense
and involved self-flagellation and the drawing of blood.

The convoy honked at people to get out of the way. Friedman likens
the moment to "someone turning on a ghetto blaster in a synagogue on
Yom Kippur, the Jewish Day of Atonement." The furious crowd threw
stones and bottles at the convoy, and the Israelis opened fire, killing two

people. In Friedman's view, the event not only revealed a shocking igno-
rance on the part of the Israelis but also provoked intensification—indeed
radicalization—of Shi'ite animosity toward their Israeli occupiers. Before
the *Ashura* incident, attacks by Shi'ites on Israelis had been sporadic, but
after it, Friedman notes, "Shi'ite clerics in south Lebanon warned that
anyone who trucked with Israel would 'burn in hell,' and Amal began
competing with other Shi'ite militias to see who could take the most Israeli casualties."[14]

The innate suspicion with which we approached clinical U.S. government intelligence was fed further by the duplicitous dealings of our government in carrying out its Middle East policy. A case in point was the
arms-for-hostages scandal, when even Prime Minister Margaret Thatcher
remained unaware of her close ally Ronald Reagan's direct bartering with
the Iranian government, in complete contradiction of his publicly stated
policy of refusing to negotiate with terrorists. A pattern of lying in public
had robbed the U.S. government of credibility.

Perhaps intelligence is by nature subject to suspicion. Terry Anderson
alluded to this when he described to me the sources for his conclusions
about Dad and the fatwa apparently issued against him. Both of Anderson's
sources were spies who worked inside Hizballah. One had been William
Buckley's agent and one had been deeply involved in the arms-for-hostages
deal. They were people whom Anderson had thoroughly "checked out"
and interviewed over the course of a year, and he believed they were credible. The information they provided to Anderson about Dad seemed plau-
sible. Yet it must be understood, Anderson emphasized in conversations we
had, that these were people who lied for a living.

It wasn't until some months later, when I read the memoir of Robert
Baer, that I understood what Terry Anderson had meant. In *See No Evil*,
Baer painted a dismaying picture of a whole underworld of intelligence
gathering in a Beirut I didn't recognize.[15] It was in a culture of suspicion
and mistrust, of rampant bugging and constantly overlapping alliances
and disputes that agents such as Baer gathered intelligence for their
bosses—in his case the CIA. Baer's depiction was reaffirmed by Magnus
Ranstorp, who told me, "In Lebanon there is a joke that everyone works
for everyone, plus five others."

In the summer of 2002, I visited New York City for the first time in many years. In Britain, I'd seen a growing tendency to stereotype insular American society, but it seemed impossible to pin such a stereotype on a place like New York, which was so fantastically international. Someone told me that 133 languages were spoken in the Bronx school district alone. My mother and I took Johan, Derek, and Willem to the United Nations and saw the famous statue of the gun with its disabled, twisted barrel. We visited the AUB head office and saw Dad's picture on the walls. We saw the shrines honoring the firefighters killed in the World Trade Center. On a visit to the USS *Intrepid* battleship museum, I bought a children's book entitled *United We Stand: America's War Against Terrorism*, which despite its alarming cover—drenched in red, white, and blue and suggesting a zealotry of its own—contained a strong message against stereotyping the outside world.[16] I came away wanting more than ever to address our experience of terrorism in my own American way.

Home again in England for the start of the new school year, our trial date was at last set for December 2002. At the same time, Bush's ultimatum to Saddam Hussein was set for early 2003. In Britain the Blair government followed suit. While bellicose threats aroused panic and protest in some quarters, confusion in the public mind mistakenly linked Iraq and September 11 and generated huge support for Bush's ultimatum.

In November, a month before our trial, my mother returned to New York for a meeting of the AUB Board of Trustees, of which she had long been a member. While there she arranged to meet with Giandomenico Picco, the former UN secretary general's negotiator whose quiet success in the years following the arms-for-hostages affair had at last brought the Western hostage crisis to a close.

Picco now ran his own consultancy but maintained close contact with former colleagues at the UN, including the Iranian delegation. He told my mother that according to his Iranian contacts, the pursuit of legal action by our family and others had spurred a continuing debate in the Iranian Parliament about the costs and benefits of state-sponsored terrorism. Legal action had played a role in making the Iranian government consider its position.

Picco advised that we should have a healthy mistrust of intelligence, which we took as a signal that somehow we were on the right track. If we were looking for the fullest and most credible picture, he said, then we must maintain the broadest base of inquiry and judge for ourselves the U.S. intelligence that fell into our hands.

He also advised that we read what he described as the definitive study of Hizballah: Magnus Ranstorp's *Hizb'allah in Lebanon*. A Swedish political scientist at the University of St. Andrew's in Scotland, Ranstorp had, according to Picco, based his investigation on extensive personal contacts within Hizballah, some of whom apparently participated in Ranstorp's seminars—a spectacular idea to say the least. Ranstorp's analysis of Hizballah activities at the time of Dad's assassination, in Picco's view, was right on the mark.

I ordered Ranstorp's book from Amazon.com and began reading the next day. It resembled the work of a social anthropologist, establishing in minute detail the vast kinship ties linking Shi'ite families who made up the Hizballah organization, the radical Shi'ite al-Dawa group in Iraq, and the clerical leaders of revolutionary Iran. In Ranstorp's portrayal of 1980s radical Shi'ism, national boundaries came second to the ancient familial ties that gave the Islamic revolution its strength. It was the awesome breadth of detail that rendered Ranstorp's conclusions credible. They were backed further, of course, by Picco's endorsement.

This setting out of familial ties was conducted alongside a practically day-by-day account of the formation of Hizballah in the first two weeks after Israel's June 6, 1982, invasion of Lebanon, the event that was the catalyst for the formal entry of Iran into Lebanon. Ranstorp described details of Iran's deal with Syria to allow the initial entry of eight hundred Iranian Revolutionary Guards into Lebanon by the Damascus-Beirut Highway, in return for nine million tons of crude oil.[17] This deal was negotiated on Iran's pretext of joining the fight against the invading Israeli Army, but Iran's true objective of establishing a foothold in Lebanon soon became clear. Indeed, Ranstorp went on to chart the Iranian Revolutionary Guard's failure, once inside Lebanon, to confront nearby Israeli Defense Forces, and instead its forceful takeover of the Lebanese National Army Barracks in Baalbek, which it quickly converted into its base of operations.[18]

It was in Baalbek that the formal Hizballah organization took root, a coming together of radical members of Amal who had split from Nabih

Berri, notably one Hussein Musawi,[19] and, with strong ideological links with members of the Iranian government itself through its ambassador to Syria, Ali Akbar Mohtashemi.[20] A Special Security Apparatus was established, responsible for intelligence and security; it was headed by Imad Mughniyeh and Abd al-Hadi Hamadi.[21] Three of these names would become associated with reports coming to our attention, from a variety of sources, that related to Dad's assassination.

Ranstorp explained the many names used by the young organization, and the reasons for them.[22] In part the variety of names reflect Hizballah's various stages of development. For example, Hussein Musawi's initial split from Nabih Berri resulted at first in his own "Islamic Amal" splinter group.[23] Cross-membership of Hizballah and al-Dawa, the Iraqi-based radical Shi'ite group, caused confusion. Individual cells within Hizballah may have had their own names. But equally, multiple names would be used by the organization when it claimed responsibility for its various acts of violence, in order to confuse Western intelligence. This kind of secrecy was in keeping with the ancient Shi'ite tradition of *taqiyya*, meaning dissimulation or concealment.[24] Islamic Jihad, the group claiming responsibility for Dad's assassination in the telephone call to Agence France-Presse on January 18, 1984, was apparently synonymous with Hizballah.[25]

Ranstorp placed Dad's assassination in what he termed as Hizballah's "Phase One" anti-Western campaign—the phase involving the elimination of principal symbolic American targets.[26] (However, he noted also that the abduction of David Dodge and Dad's assassination were undertaken as retaliatory attacks, the first coming in response to the hostage-taking of four Iranian Embassy employees,[27] and the second in response to the armed engagement of Hizballah with U.S. Marine and 6th Fleet forces.[28]) The abduction of David Dodge lasted a year but was considered a failure because no secure infrastructure for holding hostages yet existed, and the kidnappers had been forced, after several months, to transfer Dodge to an established prison in Tehran.[29] We understood as common knowledge that Syria, controlling Iran's access to Lebanon, was furious at the abduction, wanting to keep its own options open and to maintain appearances with the United States. Eventually Syria facilitated Dodge's release.[30] But the result of the fiasco was that Iran's role in the anti-American campaign was divulged. Eventually, this information would help to piece the longer story together.

While Ranstorp placed the Dodge abduction in Phase One, he considered it something of an isolated event, partly due to its failure and partly due to the fact that no more kidnappings occurred for some time. Hizballah spent the ensuing months galvanizing popular support in the three Shi'ite strongholds: the Bekaa Valley, the south, and Beirut.[31]

The next and far more spectacular acts of Phase One involved the systematic elimination of symbols of American power in Lebanon. In April 1983 came the blowing up of the political target (the U.S. Embassy), in October 1983 came the blowing up of the military target (the U.S. Marine barracks), and in January 1984 came the elimination of the cultural target (the president of the American University of Beirut). The success of Phase One is shown by the withdrawal of American multinational forces—the marines and the 6th Fleet—shortly after Dad's assassination.[32]

"Phase Two" in Ranstorp's analysis began in February 1984 and was not about eliminating large symbolic targets but about kidnappings of individuals for bargaining purposes. The need to bargain was the direct result of the convictions of twenty-one al-Dawa members in Kuwait for the attacks against the French and American Embassies there on December 12, 1983. The chief Hizballah player in the kidnapping game was Imad Mughniyeh, whose brother-in-law and cousin, Ilyas Fuad Saab, was among those convicted in Kuwait. Another prisoner in Kuwait was Hussein al-Sayed Yousef al-Musawi, a first cousin of Hizballah's Hussein Musawi.[33]

It was Ranstorp's delineation of these and further phases, based on a meticulous demonstration of intricate links in a complex system of family and clan alliances, that was for me so compelling.

Previously I could not accept that AUB had been a symbol of American cultural power perceived with the same fervent hatred that was directed at symbols of American political and military power. How could I? Perhaps I was blinded by a deep idealism that came from the American tradition of service and humanism in which I had been brought up. Far from being an arm of American political power, I saw AUB as an independent-minded institution devoted to humanistic aims of education and social welfare.

AUB Hospital had always kept its doors open to all, spending vast sums treating war casualties. If anything, AUB's outlook on Middle East politics was traditionally at odds with that of the U.S. government. It educated an Arab intellectual elite and was openly sympathetic to Arab frustrations over the Palestinian problem, which was regarded as the single most important issue in the crisis of Middle East politics.

What took so long for me to understand, and was not possible until I had looked long and hard at what revolutionary, radical Shi'ism meant, was that, as Terry Anderson said to me, "They don't care if we're journalists." Revolutionary ideology is by definition ruthless and absolute and would transcend such quibbling as to what kind of an American Dad might have been.

Ranstorp's dense, dry, and completely dispassionate rendition of these events stripped my idealistic lens away and allowed me to see Hizballah's goals for what they were. There came a sense of revelation that was almost like elation, and one day in late November 2002, I walked out into the wet countryside near my home and knew I was ready for the trial.

Excitedly, I told the rest of my family that they must get hold of copies of Ranstorp's book, but there were none to be had. Ranstorp's publisher had ordered only a small print run, and when I told Mike Martinez about the book I learned that Crowell and Moring had long bought up all the copies they could find. This book that was so novel and enlightening to me was one that our lawyers had read long before, and while this took me by surprise it also gave me a sense of reassurance. Mike suggested that Ranstorp's book could be included with the documentary evidence for the case, and so the official parameters of evidence now extended beyond the traditional world of government intelligence, to include scholarly research.

Similarly, we decided to seek a wider range of expert witnesses than had customarily been relied upon in previous cases. To supplement our lawyers' choice of Robert Oakley, the former State Department counterterrorism chief, and Patrick Clawson, the Iran specialist at the Washington-based Institute for Near East Policy, both of whom had testified in previous Hizballah cases, we sought a range of journalists, academics, and other former U.S. government officials in order to provide greater breadth and depth to our case. Terry Anderson agreed to testify; so did Richard

Murphy, former assistant secretary of state for Near East Affairs; Reginald Bartholomew, the U.S. ambassador to Lebanon at the time of Dad's assassination; William Quandt, Dad's former student and now a Middle East specialist at the University of Virginia; and David Dodge. Thomas Friedman also agreed, and we began to make arrangements for his testimony, until his employer intervened. Three or four other diplomats and academics were sought but, like Friedman's boss, felt their professional independence would be compromised if they participated in a lawsuit of this nature.

Six weeks or so before the trial date, a few hundred pages of documentation came spewing forth as a result of our Freedom of Information Act applications. There was still no raw intelligence pertaining directly to Dad's murder, but the documents were nonetheless chilling. Most of them were reports by U.S. intelligence in Beirut about Dad's activities during his eighteen months as AUB president. This perspective—that of Dad's own government watching him—was unexpected, but it fit the emerging sketch of the world he had stepped into.

Although what they disclosed was not pleasant, doors kept opening to reveal the world in which Dad had died.

We flew to Washington and I felt a sense of confidence and satisfaction in the evidence to be presented to the court. I did not expect to learn anything new, since it seemed that we had now completed our work.

The day before the opening of the trial my mother, brothers, and I sat in the Crowell and Moring office going over plans for the next day. We previewed the video deposition of Ambassador Bartholomew and met with Robert Oakley, who would testify the next day. These were people who had worked for the government, and I had long since pegged them in my mind as predictable witnesses.

But just as the reading of Ranstorp's dispassionate account of radical revolutionary Shi'ism had produced an overwhelming sense of understanding, now these two ex-federal employees provided equally revelatory dimensions to the story—again, so obvious once seen. What each had to say related to Dad's position in Arab society as someone regarded as a friend—someone who was working for and not against the Arab and Islamic worlds.

Oakley and Bartholomew suggested answers to two nagging questions we had tried to shrug off: Why had Dad been killed when all other individual human targets had been kidnapped? Why hadn't Dad's affinity and affection for Lebanon afforded him some protection?

Oakley's answer to the first question was that at the time, an infrastructure for successful kidnapping of high profile targets did not exist. There was no reliable and secure system of prisons, guards, and transport of prisoners. The release of the one hostage before Dad—David Dodge— had been considered a failure for the abductors, and several of those kidnapped in the months immediately after Dad's assassination would manage to escape.[34] More important, Oakley proposed, Dad as a hostage would have angered many factions, and they would have gone looking for him. He would have been too difficult to hold, Oakley argued. And so he was literally eliminated.

As to the second question, Bartholomew explained his personal conviction that there were two reasons for Dad's assassination. One was that which we had come to accept—that he was a victim in a campaign to eliminate Westerners. The other reason, ironically, had to do precisely with his recognized affinity for Lebanon. Dad had somehow crossed the line in revolutionary Iran's portrait of the demon enemy, and that created a special need to remove him. This was a view that Andrew, years before, had suggested. At the time I dismissed it as preposterous, but now it began to make sense to me.

Years before when I had ventured even slightly to find out what on earth had happened to Dad, I'd always been told, "You will never know." It was true that no one was ever going to sit down and tell me definitively exactly what had happened to Dad—how long the gunmen had watched his patterns before fixing the hour of death, whether they knew he would be going to the bank on his way to the office that morning, whether one or both of them fired bullets, and whether indeed they passed my mother as they fled through the nearest gate out of the campus a few minutes later, as she thinks they might have. Finding the essence of the truth in a way we could have faith in took time and initiative, but it was possible. What I had learned made the broad outlines of the story more complex than I had ever imagined them to be, but equally, more understandable.

The identity of the bearer of the gun was secondary to me. My stance was against state-sponsored killing and the incitement thereof. I understood now that lawlessness created ideal conditions for sponsored violence, and therefore my stance was also in support of the rule of law. The weight of evidence pointed overwhelmingly in the direction of Iran and Hizballah, and I felt a moral responsibility to pursue legal justice.

The final words completing the story belonged to Dad. Some of them were in the old cardboard box in the attic, after all.

.   .   .

A year after the trial the U.S. government released a document under the Freedom of Information Act that none of us had seen before. It clearly identified the group responsible for Dad's assassination and verified the whole of the case presented to the court on our behalf. It also revealed that our government had known the identity of those responsible within three weeks of Dad's assassination. It took us only twenty years to find out.[35]

6

Words Remembered

IN 1956, the year he married my mother, twenty-six-year-old Malcolm
Kerr embarked on a Ph.D. dissertation that addressed the dilemma of
how, in the secular age of the early twentieth century, two Egyptian intel-
lectuals had sought a meaningful application of Islam.

He wrote his dissertation at Harvard, under the tutelage of the great
British Islamicist Sir Hamilton Gibb. While he worked in the small apartment on Ware Street that he shared with my mother, she went out to teach
at Newton Junior High School. It was on Ware Street, they loved to tell me,
that I was conceived.

In the fall of 1958 the dissertation was complete, and my parents
moved to Lebanon. My paternal grandparents still lived in Beirut, a
few floors down from my parents' own apartment in the lovely Jurdak
Building overlooking the Mediterranean Sea. Dad began his first teaching job at AUB, and my mother gave birth to me, and then two years
later to John.

Dad often said that those were the happiest years of his life. It was
with regret that they decided eventually to leave Beirut for a job at UCLA,
so that their children could grow up in their country of citizenship. First
however came a study leave in Oxford, where a life-long friendship with
another great scholar and mentor, Albert Hourani, took root and where
Dad revised his dissertation.

This chapter contains extracts taken from unpublished personal and professional correspondence between Malcolm Kerr and his family and colleagues, all of which passed into
my possession at the time of his death.

With my parents on the balcony of our apartment in the Jurdak Building, Beirut, 1960. My grandparents lived in a flat downstairs from us.

Eventually published under the title *Islamic Reform,* Dad's first book was respected in academic circles for its command of the Arabic sources, and for what, thirty-five years later, a Lebanese colleague described in a memorial tribute as "its mental transposition"—the ability to comprehend the Islamic system of life from the inside.[1]

Dad's greatest professional acclaim would result from his next book, a study of inter-Arab politics of the 1950s and 1960s entitled *The Arab Cold War*—a concise work composed in three months and published three times, of which the most often quoted words came from the preface to the third edition, in which he lamented that "Arab politics has ceased to be fun." His analogy of the June 1967 war as a disastrous Princeton football game went down in history, capturing for his American readership that vital sense of common ground across history and cultures.[2]

Over the next two dozen years, the dramas of inter-Arab politics carried on, recognition of Israel was made by one or two Arab leaders, and the disaster of the unresolved Palestine question passed through many chapters. We spent a year in Cairo, where John and I attended the Franciscan nuns' school and found ourselves fluent in French within a few weeks. The next year we were back in Beirut, where Steve was born. Andrew followed three years later, when we had returned to life in California. Dad continued to write on the key issues of the day, observing unfolding history with growing concern.

His last book, a jointly edited volume entitled *Rich and Poor States in the Middle East*, contained his famous scenarios for the future of the Arab world, and his characterization of the new Islamic Iran's virulent xenophobia and punitive hostility. "We shall omit," he wrote, "one scenario whose potential importance cannot be denied: the 'doomsday' case of a war in the Gulf [that] . . . involves so many worldwide as well as local ramifications that it is a better subject for a whole book."[3]

Dad died long before that doomsday scenario began to play itself out. But the issue he sought to understand as a twenty-six-year-old proved, for him personally and for global politics generally, to be one of equal magnitude: the application of Islam in a modern, secular world. Malcolm Kerr was exactly halfway through his short life when he produced that fateful first book. How did he himself become a victim of the unresolved dilemma about which he wrote? Why did he agree to become a player on the historical stage when he suspected, as he confided to me one terrible night, that he had "a fifty-fifty chance of getting bumped off?"

■   ■   ■

A dozen years before Dad came into the world, twenty-four-year-old Stanley Kerr sat down in the town of Marash, Turkey, to compose a farewell letter to his parents. A few hours later, French occupation troops would abandon the town, leaving behind its orphaned and elderly Armenian residents in anticipation of a devastating siege by Turkish Nationalists. Into the freezing night of February 9, 1920, those Armenians who were able would accompany the retreating French. "Many will perish on the way, from Turkish bullets and from cold," Stanley wrote. He and the other men and women of the American Committee for Near East Relief would stay behind to protect the orphans and the elderly. "If the Turks do not respect our flag and property we will die with the others. . . . No matter

Baby Malcolm in his mother Elsa's arms, with sisters Marion and Dorothy, and father, Stanley, at home in Beirut, 1932.

what happens remember that I am ready to make any sacrifice even death, and have no fear. We all realize that we are in God's care and are trusting in him absolutely. My only regret if I die is that I won't be able to work for you and Dad to make your days happy, after all the sacrifices you have made for me to make my life count for something."

Stanley concluded his letter by restating his love for his family, and issuing a warning to his government about the responsibilities of power: "May this horror of these last weeks be a blot on the pages of history, both of France and America for their part in delaying the peace of Turkey. And may America, as a result of this, take a more unselfish attitude about a protectorate for this country."

While Dad's life ended with his role on the historical stage, Stanley's life thus began. Stanley's declaration of service to the people of Marash, where two years later he was to court my grandmother, evolved into a life's work at the American University of Beirut. It was that world, with those values, into which Stanley and Elsa's four children were born and grew up, and in which eventually my father would meet my mother. And while the most prominent risk to fifty-two-year-old Malcolm Kerr happened to be the politics of radical Islam, the secular nationalism that caused the violent expulsion of Turkey's Armenians before young Stanley's eyes was to prove an equally potent ingredient in the explosive struggles of a post–World War I Middle East that dominated, and outlived, the century shared by father and son. So, too, endured the matter that Stanley so angrily pointed out: the responsibilities of the Allied Powers in "delaying the peace."

．　．　．

Dad's portable typewriter, the laptop of his day, traveled the world with us. Whether we were living in the mountains of Lebanon, the suburbs of Cairo, a fishing village in Tunisia, or a cottage in southern France, Dad would set up the typewriter and roll the sandwich of carbon and white paper into it in order to produce duplicate copies of whatever he was busy writing—observations of a recent trip, letters to his parents, or drafts of a new book. Always I marveled at his ability as a typist, going on and on without making a single mistake, and loved the sound of the typewriter blended together with his favorite Mozart opera or piano concerto.

The subjects of his books were terribly serious in contrast to the funny, warm man we knew. They were also diverse, and Dad managed to cover a wide range of subjects without losing his passion. There was only one exception, when instead of a year in Jerusalem and the Arab world, my parents decided to spend our sabbatical year in the French town of Aix-en-Provence. Dad wrote to his parents that he and my mother had decided to try something new, partly because he was afraid of "drowning in the Arab-Israeli problem." Narrow specialization carried the risk of stunted intellectual growth, and that he wished to avoid.

But Dad's project for the year in Aix, a study of education in North Africa, never really took off, and he found himself frustrated at being away from the Middle East at a time when so many momentous events were taking place. I remember the look on his face when the BBC World Service announced that Gamal 'Abd al-Nasser, the principal subject of *The Arab Cold War*, had died suddenly in Egypt. That year, 1970, was also the year that King Hussein expelled the militant Palestinian leadership from Jordan, and that the PLO established itself anew in Lebanon. Dad spent many hours typing letters to Stanley and Elsa, now retired in Princeton and his confidantes in matters of Middle East politics, expressing his frustrations and airing strong views about recent events.

Nevertheless, my parents had planned another summer in the mountains of Lebanon in advance of that year in France, and while we were in Ainab, Dad sneaked off with a second passport and made a nine-day trip to "Dixieland," as the land south of the border was known. Dad had spent a few months in Jerusalem as a nine-year-old boy when his family fled Lebanon in 1940, but this was his first trip to Israel. He was eager to see firsthand a place he had spent so much time trying to understand. He wanted, he said, to "try and learn what has been going on since 1967, and especially, what the Israelis really want."

The trip was shorter than he would have liked, but still Dad came away armed with his own perception of the Israelis as people, as opposed to what he called "conditioned" perceptions acquired by years of living in Beirut. At the same time, his conviction of the moral injustice underlying the Israeli state was reaffirmed, depending as it did on the displacement of another people. So was the "terrible failure of American leaders to really try to understand the Arabs." It was intensely troubling to him that "the best people are perfectly capable of carrying on the worst policies. Conversely, the people with the most reasonable case can botch it and put themselves in the wrong, or seem to."

It was this quest to learn firsthand about "what people really want" that was so characteristic of Dad. His writings, and indeed his actions as a person, were underpinned by a sense of empathy, and it was a quality shared by my mother. It meant many study leaves in many new countries, for they believed that the best way to learn about people was to learn from experience. For us children, it meant attending new schools and having to learn a new language, though this was not something we necessarily enjoyed. In Aix, Dad spent hours each evening shepherding me through my mountains of homework in French, rather than reading and writing and breaking into his new project. But that was all part of the package.

Indeed Dad's empathy was not sentimental, but concerned and critical. He wanted the best for people, and that meant working for it. He expressed this approach around the time of that year in France, in a two-page foreword to a collection of essays edited by Ibrahim Abu-Lughod entitled *The Arab-Israeli Confrontation of June 1967: An Arab Perspective*. Dad was the only non-Arab contributor to the volume. Some, in hasty judgment, might cite this as evidence of Dad's partisanship, but in fact his words are far more interesting and provocative if taken seriously, as surely they were intended:

> We hear much today about the pitfalls of being culture-bound. Our perceptions of the world are distorted not only by the incompleteness of our information but also by the way in which our established habits of thought and taste and our inherited forms of moral preference tend to mold our consciousness of events into familiar patterns. The truly cultivated man is marked by empathy—by his recognition that the thought and understanding of men of other cultures may differ sharply from his own, that what seems natural to him may appear grotesque to others, and that each pattern without the complement of the others is parochial.[4]

A couple of years later, Dad became one of the early presidents of the Middle East Studies Association. As such he was required to deliver an opening address at the annual gathering, that year in Binghamton, New York. His speech was a typical mixture of jokes (concluding with one about Egyptian hell being preferable to Soviet heaven) and utterly serious remarks. He spoke at length about the dangers of human insensitivity in international politics, evoking the words of Arnold Toynbee fifty years before when he issued a prophetic warning of the fallout of Western cultural imperialism in the Middle East: "Should not we turn our head and move out of the light before our victims stagger to their feet and stab us in the back?"[5]

It shocks me now to think of the grave and worrying thoughts that preoccupied him at a time when he was of course simply a father. When he came home from these trips—and usually we had no idea where he'd been—my mother would drop all four of us children at the curb at the airport and wait with the car while we tore into the terminal building, racing up the corridor until we spotted Dad walking down from the gate.

. . .

By then Dad had reached the pinnacle of his career at UCLA, having become dean of Social Sciences. Yet he was ever painfully distant from the Arab world at a time when the fortunes of its people were becoming only more critical. The horrific murders of Israeli athletes at the 1972 Olympics in Munich did nothing to cultivate sympathy for the Palestinian cause. Another disastrous Arab-Israeli war erupted in 1973, and in 1975 the imbalanced politics of Lebanon's myriad sectarian groups saw the beginning of its long and bloody civil war. In America, anti-Arab sentiment only grew as people sat in their cars lining up at gas stations during the oil embargo of 1973–74.

A job prospect at AUB came into view but was for some reason deemed unsuitable and I, having inherited my parents' strong attachment to the Middle East, cried so long that I had to stay home from school until my puffy eyes returned to normal.

At last another sabbatical year was due, and we all set off for Cairo in 1976. For me, a freshman year at the American University in Cairo plugged me into Dad's world in a way I hadn't experienced before. I was unabashedly proud and happy riding to AUC with him in the mornings and listening to his answers to my questions at the dinner table in the evenings. In the middle of that year, food riots erupted when the Egyptian government reduced subsidies on basic goods. A curfew was imposed, and after a few days we were finally allowed to go out of our apartment. We saw the overturned, burned-out cars in the streets, and for the first time I learned something about essential grievances that make people desperate and angry.

At Oberlin College, where I continued after that first year at AUC, I enrolled in Arabic and Middle Eastern history classes. I loved Arabic and threw myself into its beautiful script. But unfolding history—particularly the continuing civil war in Lebanon and the Iranian Revolution—overwhelmed me. One day I read in *Newsweek* that a journalist friend of my parents, Joe Alex Morris, had been killed that week by a sniper in Tehran.

His eldest daughter was about my age. I felt paralyzed with grief and furious at the sterile manner in which the news had been imparted. I dropped the Middle Eastern history course I'd just signed up for, which I was sure could never explain to me why such a thing had happened.

The return to California was hard for both my parents, and they found a way of returning to Cairo in 1979, where they spent two more years happily situated. My mother studied for her master's degree at AUC and Dad found his niche among the Egyptian colleagues with whom he collaborated on *Rich and Poor States in the Middle East*.

Cairo became our second home in the Arab world. And from Cairo there were other places to go as well: everyone came to visit me when I taught at St. George's School in Jerusalem the year after I graduated from college, and we ventured to Lebanon now and then, becoming accustomed to the sound of gunfire and the slowly eroding landscape. Even so, stepping off the plane in Beirut and heading to Ainab or to stay with friends at AUB was electrifying: it was a place where Dad felt complete and where both he and my mother felt a sense of overwhelming possibility, and those feelings were contagious.

But that sojourn came to an end in 1981, and when my parents returned as due to UCLA, they discovered that they'd moved on and were ready for other things. I remember, too, Dad confiding one evening that perhaps he didn't want to write any more books. He said simply, "Writing is hard." This surprised me because the hum of his typewriter had been so steady for as long as I could remember. But perhaps it was somehow reassuring, too. We were all finding our way in those days.

· · ·

Even before my parents had left Cairo, rumors of new job prospects had floated around. The most enticing rumor was of the AUB presidency, and so when Dad was asked if he would like to be considered for another job in Cairo, he declined, preferring to gamble on the one for which he secretly hoped. The fact that AUB had had to survive and indeed develop against the backdrop of civil war perhaps added to the enticement—not for any perverse thrill in the face of danger but because the sense of mission upon which AUB was founded inspired new commitment.

At home in California, Christmas 1982, all in new AUB sweatshirts: John, Andrew, Ann, Malcolm, Susan, and Steve.

Dad was at that time a trustee of AUB, which meant regular trips to New York for meetings of the board. I was enrolled in a master's program at Harvard, still taken up with all things Arabic and Islamic but a bit wiser after the year in East Jerusalem, where I'd witnessed firsthand the daily realities of the Arab-Israeli conflict. In November and March, I would take the train down from Boston to New York and meet Dad at the Roosevelt Hotel, where he stayed during AUB board meetings. Once I arrived before he did and was tucked up in bed by the time he finally showed up. "Let's go down to the bar!" he suggested, and we did.

On the third weekend of March 1982, still on that cusp of life that precedes the responsibilities of adulthood, I met Dad at the Roosevelt again. But this time was different: the trustees had narrowed down their search for a new president to two candidates, Dad and David Dodge. Both were products of an AUB childhood, and David was already the university's vice-president. The two old friends spent that Saturday waiting together while the trustees mulled over their decision, scrutinizing among other things Dad's outspoken writings and speculating as to their potential repercussions.

I wonder if they had read Dad's editorial in the *Los Angeles Times* of the week before. It described the near inevitability of an Israeli invasion of Lebanon, and soon, for the purpose of "smashing" the PLO. This was a goal that might entail the outrageous scenario of an Israeli occupation of West Beirut. Such an invasion was certain to provoke immediate and dangerous international repercussions, with Syria, the Soviet Union, Iraq, and Jordan forced to respond somehow. The Israeli press had openly discussed the possibility of such an invasion, believing that Menachem Begin's government simply awaited Palestinian provocation, which journalists insisted was "only a matter of time."[6]

Meanwhile, Dad felt it was likely he would be chosen for the job at AUB. That night in our hotel room we talked about the pros and cons of such a prospect. It would mean for us all giving up a whole way of life in Los Angeles. There were endless practicalities to consider, including the fact that Steve would not want to give up his final year on the high school basketball team. But looking at the bigger picture, it was hard for either Dad or me to suppress our excitement at the prospect of a job that was something of a dream come true.

Certainly I hadn't read Dad's editorial, and we talked about all the reasons why the situation in Lebanon might improve. I was ready to hear anything positive, though I don't think I really understood the basic outlines of what was going on in Lebanon. Perhaps Dad was pinning hope on the refusal of the U.S. government, as paymaster to the Israeli Defense Forces, to allow any Israeli incursion into Lebanon. Everyone knew that AUB symbolized hope in Lebanon, with every faction in the civil war represented in the student body. As I had seen with my own eyes, AUB had remained off limits in the civil war, and life inside its walls was peaceful and even idyllic.

"Do you think I should go?" Dad asked, and I was shocked and honored that he wanted my opinion. I felt sure that AUB was the place for him, and, caught up in the drama of this conversation, I must have been seized by a sense of idealism. But as soon as I told him I thought he should go, I fell off that cusp of life that stands at the edge of true adulthood. For after we turned out the lights and said goodnight, I heard Dad's clear and sober voice: "I bet there's a fifty-fifty chance I'll get bumped off early on."

I can't help but look back, analyzing every word of what we said to each other after that bombshell shattered the quiet of our hotel room. I know we told each other all the things one would wish to have said to a loved one only when it is too late. It was as though we actually said good-bye, as though the decision had already been made, as though fate had somehow overtaken us. I can't explain why the next morning Dad accepted the job, except that it was a decision that had been years in the making. My own overwhelming memory of that terrible acknowledgment of the worst-case scenario fills every corner of my mind, blotting out the bigger picture. I held Dad tight when I met him at noon the next day and he asked, "How would you like to hug the next president of AUB?"

. . .

Dad always had insightful things to say about what was going on in the Middle East, and even something to say about what might happen next. He seemed to have an answer to every question I ever asked. And yet I have to accept the fact that he wasn't a crystal ball. The Iranian factor was only still evolving that weekend in March 1982, and although Dad had already described with deadly accuracy the Iranian "punitive hostility" of which he would one day be a recipient, he had not foreseen its imminent manifestation in Lebanon, nor indeed himself as its target.

Had he been away from Lebanon too long to anticipate that scenario? Or was it too soon to be seen? Did he think he knew where the risks lay, and that he could outwit them?

Dad agreed to stop writing newspaper editorials when he accepted the job at AUB, and so there is little to go back to now to discover what he was thinking about during those tense months between late March and early June, when we all counted on the best-case scenario winning out. Dad was due to take up the job on July 1, and he and my mother had turned their attention to practical matters, including the decision that she and Andrew would stay behind in Los Angeles that first year so that Steve could complete his final year in high school, where he was now a star on the basketball team.

On the evening of June 3, all of us were at home in California, sitting around the dining-room table, when the telephone rang. I can't remember who called to tell us that the Israeli ambassador in London had just been shot. This act was the trigger that set into motion all the events that culminated in Dad's assassination eighteen months later. I do remember the looks on my parents' faces, as though they had just glimpsed their own future.

The Israeli invasion of Lebanon began three days later. Palestinians and Shi'ites in the south fled northward, and a devastating aerial bombardment of Beirut began. The Reagan administration refused to condemn publicly the invasion by a military machine openly financed by U.S. taxpayers, causing anti-American sentiment to erupt where before it had not existed. A multinational peacekeeping force consisting of Italian, French, and American units arrived in Lebanon and had to learn the intricacies of this complex war as it went along.

According to Ranstorp, within two weeks into the invasion, the Lebanese National Salvation Committee was formed by President Sarkis in an attempt to pull together in the face of a common enemy. Nabih Berri, leader of the Shi'ite faction Amal, decided to join. Berri was condemned by radical Amal members for having abandoned the Islamic revolutionary aims of sections of his community. And while Berri was condemned, his deputy, Hussein Musawi, a man who espoused the now crystallizing vision of an Islamic revolution in Lebanon, became its champion.[7]

The Israeli invasion was the central event in Lebanon at the time, and the Iranian factor now began to play out as one of its chief by-products. All the other by-products of that invasion, but chiefly the intense disaffection of Lebanon's Shi'ites and Palestinians, enhanced the opportunities for success in fostering the Islamic revolution. Shi'ites and Palestinians were forced out of the south and then bombed in Beirut, and they lacked effective leadership to protect them.

Animosity toward Israel induced by the invasion, as well as toward the United States for its unwillingness to challenge Israel's forward march, signaled to Iran that the time to enter Lebanon was right. It was at that point, on the pretext of joining forces against the invading Israelis, that Iran persuaded Syria (with the added inducement of promises of annual oil shipments) to allow entry into Lebanon of a large contingent of Iranian Revolutionary Guards. One of its first actions was the forceful takeover of the Lebanese National Army barracks in the ancient city of Baalbek. This barracks was transformed into Iranian headquarters in Lebanon.

Within two or three weeks of the Israeli invasion, Iran thus established its foothold in Lebanon, absorbing into its chain of command Hussein Musawi and other radical elements in Lebanon's Shi'ite hierarchy and forming together a new movement eventually known as Hizballah, meaning "Party of God." Hizballah was dedicated to the forceful implementation of the Islamic revolution in Lebanon. Essential to Hizballah's goal was the removal of Westerners from Lebanese soil. Hizballah's first attack in conjunction with its anti-Western objective was the kidnapping of the president of AUB.

But Dad was not in Beirut. He was at the AUB head office in New York, where he and my mother spent the summer watching and waiting while Lebanon unraveled. I stayed with my brothers at home in Los Angeles. David Dodge, already in Lebanon when the invasion began, stayed on at AUB as acting president until Dad could make his way to Beirut. David communicated back and forth with the New York office by telex, listing casualties taken in by the AUB Hospital and reporting on direct hits to the campus and trying to gauge where they were coming from. "God bless and keep thee safe and sane," Najeeb Halaby, AUB's chairman of the board, telexed back as the momentum of attacks increased.

On July 19, David was thrown into the trunk of a car in the heart of the presumably untouchable AUB campus, and for all intents and purposes disappeared into thin air. If it had been impossible for Dad to turn back before, now the screws tightened: in addition to the certain knowledge of deadly risk was the terrible fact that someone else had taken the first hit in his place. It was Joe Alex Morris's widow, Ulla, who broke the news to me, in a way that helped me to keep a grip as our nightmare unfolded.

By early August, that new and growing anti-American sentiment was approaching a point of no return. A Lebanese trustee of AUB, Salwa Es-Said, telexed an imploring warning to the New York office:

> After yesterday's demential slaughter of Beirut's population, I want to make it quite clear that the attitude of the U.S. is incomprehensible. Those of us who have been supporting the U.S. can no longer do so as long as the U.S. government can tolerate such barbarous activities. The hatred that has been generated is going

to overflow onto the campus. We may not be able to preserve the integrity of our campus, or the safety of its staff. People are homeless and without water. Do you know what it means to be thirsty?

In case there is a black-out on our Lebanese news, as is often the case, let me brief you: the Israeli raids started yesterday at dawn and shelled non-stop until 5 P.M. by sea, land and air at the rate of three shells per second. No residential building was spared. The Makassed and Barbir Hospitals, two of the most important Lebanese hospitals, were badly damaged. One surgeon lost his leg while attending to his patients. The homeless in Beirut have tripled in number in the last few days.

I ask you to intervene in the strongest possible way, and at the highest possible level, to safe-guard whatever credibility is left toward the U.S. and salvage the AUB, perhaps the most distinguished U.S. endeavor in the Middle East.

A week later, fully attuned to the utter transformation of his new job, Dad composed a letter to Samir Thabet, a Lebanese administrator holding down the fort at AUB in the wake of David Dodge's kidnapping. I found the carbon copy tucked away among those pages of frantic telexes, many years later, and was almost reassured when I read it. Although by August 1982 we had all moved to new and strange states of mind, Dad was obviously governed by a sure sense of professionalism and knew exactly how he wanted to proceed.

Dear Samir,

As Nuhad Dagher will be returning to Beirut soon, I am taking the opportunity to write you a few personal lines on this battered old typewriter. I feel that communications have been difficult at best for us this summer. Essential information is conveyed well enough by telex, but what is not conveyed very well is personal feeling, which is sometimes a most important commodity.

I want you and my other friends there to know that I am deeply conscious of the terribly difficult position you have been in, very unhappy with my own status here in exile, and well aware that it is natural for people in Beirut to make invidious comparisons between their own situation and mine, and to ask why I am not with them. Your position is much the worse of the two: I may worry a bit about my reputation, you must worry about your life, and furthermore you have an extremely trying and thankless job under miserable living conditions, plus the knowledge that when the nonsense is finally over, Kerr will grandly arrive and take over in keeping with his own convenience. I would expect this to be a most irritating situation for you to put up with, and believe me, I greatly dislike it, and wish it were not so.

I suppose the simplest thing would be for me just to declare that my time is more profitably spent in the U.S. during the crisis, fund raising etcetera. This is true enough in itself. Again, I think it can be said that were I in Beirut I would cause people a major headache trying to arrange my safety. However, there is no denying that for me and probably for most of those who have been advising me, the overwhelming consideration is that little could in fact be done to provide security and that as a newly arrived American full president of AUB I would be a prime target. I think you know very well that if I were already there, I would not leave. Conversely, if you had just been appointed as Vice President, I do not think it would make sense for you to come just yet. All this is miserable logic from the standpoint of those who are in Beirut now, but pretty compelling nonetheless when it comes to making a practical decision.

I am truly anxious to get to Beirut at the first reasonable moment and feel that with the optimism of an evacuation agreement in the news these days, the time is not far off. By the time this reaches you we will know more. My thought is that once the Lebanese security forces have entered West Beirut I should leave here as soon as I can get packed up, i.e. a few days. I would at that point be looking for a telex or phone call from you giving your appraisal of the security situation, and of course I will consult Najeeb Halaby, my wife, and perhaps Ambassador Dillon. But my guiding principle will be that my job is in Beirut, that people are waiting for me to show up with some legitimate impatience, and that my arrival should be at the first reasonable moment. And at the first reasonable moment thereafter, it will be time for you to take an extended holiday far away from Lebanon. The same goes for the Deans and others.

I wish I knew what to say about poor David. He is constantly on my mind. He has been a good friend since I was a teen-ager, and I cannot conceive of a personality more deserving of a better fate, totally unselfish and driven by duty and good will. Since I was here safely installed in New York, it was he rather than I who paid the price. You can imagine how I feel about that.

Samir, I don't suppose under the circumstances there is any escaping a certain margin of strain or resentment or loss of confidence that will be directed against me by people at AUB. I take it for granted that this is built into the psychological environment. It will be a burden for me to carry after I arrive. I accept this and am prepared to face it as a fact of life. On an emotional level I confess to feeling quite guilty about it, though not on a rational level since I believe I have done the only reasonable thing. If you or others do agree with me, or at least respect my reasoning, on a rational level, then I do ask that you help me minimize the damage as far as you are able to do so. I do have a job that needs to be done well for everyone's sake and I am going to give it my best shot, hoping thereby to make up for lost momentum and to earn the respect of all of you who have been spared.

Please convey my affectionate and admiring greetings to all our colleagues, and please accept them for yourself. I am looking forward to being with you soon.

As ever,
Malcolm

But it was the American ambassador to Lebanon, Robert Dillon, who made the first move on the subject of the right time for Dad to go. And although Dad was sure of what he wanted to do for AUB, the rest of us would have supported him had he decided instead to endure the terrible humiliation of giving it all up. He could not look any of us in the eye when Ambassador Dillon telephoned on August 17 instructing him in no uncertain terms to make his way directly to Beirut or risk losing the respect of the AUB community for good.

With Beirut International Airport closed, Dad flew to Cyprus to find transportation to Beirut. He arrived in Lebanon by private yacht, the *Sea Victory*, with all the bizarre incongruities that are the hallmark of war. A gourmet dinner was followed by a James Bond video, and then Dad slept on deck, glad to have the Chinese air mattress he'd bought at the army-navy store in Los Angeles. I can't help but smile when I imagine it refusing to deflate the next morning, as he told us it did. As the yacht approached the harbor of Jounieh it was detained by an Israeli gunship, and the passengers were treated to another video, this time *The Sound of Music*. Finally the boat docked, and Dad made his way up to Baabda, a Christian enclave on the outskirts of East Beirut.

He began writing letters to his family from the moment he arrived, trying to reassure us but helping us imagine his surroundings, too. He wrote little or nothing of the radical transformation of the Shi'ite community, about which I tried so hard to learn so many years later. Instead, Dad described what he witnessed out of his windows and what he heard in the distance. In those first few weeks, the picture changed almost daily, with the forced evacuation of the PLO, the Israeli takeover of West Beirut, the assassination of president-elect Bashir Gemayel, and the massacres of Palestinians and Shi'ites at the Sabra and Shatila refugee camps.

Dad did not look back when he stepped on to the deck at Jounieh. His guiding principles, his sense of humor, and his cool-headedness helped him to rise to the occasion and keep his feet firmly on the ground.

．　■　．

Baabda
September 1, 1982
Dear Mother,

I am writing from the house of my friends Elie and Phyllis Salem in a suburb outside Beirut. I arrived here last Saturday after spending two days in Amman and 24 hours in Cyprus, and sailing from the latter to Jounieh aboard an Englishman's private yacht, along with 16 other paying passengers! The trip overnight from Cyprus was quite nice except for having to sleep on deck, plus the fact that an Israeli gunboat came alongside to inspect us and made us wait three or four hours before allowing us to enter Lebanese waters. Evidently Lebanon's waters, not to mention her skies, are now Israeli property. On finally arriving in Jounieh and getting off the boat, I was surprised to find that there was nobody there to meet me, so I took a taxi to the U.S. Ambassador's residence for a $40 fee and threw myself on the mercy of the embassy personnel there. Before long I had a swim in the Ambassador's private pool and my friends the Salems came to pick me up, and I got over my complex about being stranded at the dock.

For the first three days I stayed away from Ras Beirut since it was considered somewhat risky to go there, what with the PLO evacuation going on and the armed groups there feeling jumpy about Bashir Gemayel being elected president. The Salems took me up to the Ainab hilltop and we wound up staying overnight. The Israeli army occupies the top of the hill near the gunroad, and apparently doesn't behave particularly well, having frequent aimless shooting matches with the neighboring rocks, trees, and villagers. Some of the trees in the Ainab woods have been clipped off by gunfire. Also some houses in the village were wrecked by shellfire, but it is not as bad as I had feared.

Yesterday I hitched a ride in a U.S. Embassy car, escorted by Lebanese riot police, to the AUB campus and stayed overnight in Marquand House. This entailed crossing from east to west Beirut at the Museum and driving through interminable alleys and small streets through terrible devastation from the Israeli bombing and shelling; and today when we returned by a different route I saw even worse specimens of devastation. Here and there were occasional squads of French and Italian soldiers, part of the international peacekeeping force—the U.S. marines are at the harbor, which I haven't seen yet. I would say that the eastern and southern sectors of Beirut, which were not shelled by the Israelis, look quite clean and very prosperous, whereas the west Beirut neighborhoods look much worse than anything in the slums of major cities in the US, with their caved-in buildings, the rubble, the garbage, and the congestion. The AUB neighborhood has not really been hit but it is very shabby. Today the final group of the PLO left Beirut, and we heard gunfire continuously from the AUB campus as the friends of the PLO emptied their ammunition into the air in salute. Apparently a lot of people have been killed so far by stray bullets from the shots fired in celebration.

I came back to the Salems' house in the afternoon but will return to AUB tomorrow to settle in. Life there is very quiet and there is no reason to fear for one's safety. The armed groups that had infested the campus throughout the summer have all left. I do have a local boy walking around with me as a bodyguard, and I only venture out on the streets with a carload of police, but I don't think these precautions will be needed for more than a few weeks. This morning, my first day at the office, I presided over a meeting of the Board of Deans at which we discussed the David Dodge situation—there isn't much we can do—and the question of what date we would announce for the opening of classes in the fall. We decided to postpone classes for a week after the initially scheduled date to give people a chance to get back to some sort of normal existence and for the faculty to return from abroad. So we will begin October 21.

One very curious thing I have learned in my few days here so far is that a great many people in Lebanon were so fed up with the PLO and its antics that they have actually regarded the Israeli army as saviors, even though the Israelis destroyed half of Beirut in the process. Not that the Israelis are popular per se, but the PLO and their friends are the object of unbelievable hostility, and not only from right wing Christians but also from Moslems. I am getting a new perspective on a number of things in this regard. Most particularly it puts the election of Bashir Gemayel in a different light. He has a background as a thug and a bully, but many people see him as the embodiment of Lebanon's only chance to return to some kind of sanity. Right now it does look as if the situation in Beirut will return to quasi-normality, although no one is so sure that the same will be the case in the Bekaa or in Tripoli, where large numbers of PLO and Syrians are still entrenched.

I'm going to have to get used to being a bachelor. I have already decided that I definitely do not like eating meals by myself, other than breakfast, and I expect to compensate for my plight by inviting a succession of friends and colleagues to have lunch and dinner with me at Marquand House. Tomorrow Kamal Salibi is coming. He told me on the phone today that Usama Khalidi is in bed with a jaw operation. It seems Usama phoned Kamal and said, "I have bad news and good news. The bad news is that I have a jaw infection and have to have an operation that will keep me in bed for weeks. The good news is that I won't be able to open my mouth and you won't have to listen to me."

Sorry about my typing. This is an electric typewriter and I'm not used to it. Besides, the light is very poor and I can hardly see what I am writing.

More later. It's now 10:15 and I should go to bed. Outside the house I can hear the roar of Israeli tanks parading down the street just outside the Salems' house here in Baabda. They have made this suburb their headquarters and they and their huge tanks and artillery pieces are all over the place. Who would ever have thought the Israelis would be in occupation of places like Baabda, or Aley and Ainab?

Love,
Mac

Marquand House
September 11, 1982
Dear Susie and John,

I've been installed here on campus for ten days now and am getting used to the idea of being the Lord of the Manor, though I do miss having the Lady and all the little Lordlets around as well. I've been playing tennis every two or three days, have been jogging a couple of times, and am just waiting till the day after tomorrow when the AUB swimming beach is supposed to open up. I have also had numerous friends over to hang around the Marquand House garden with me for lunch, dinner, etc. In the meantime life here is very tranquil. I am rattling around all by myself among the five bedrooms on the second floor (one of which I am using for my study) while on the ground floor there is nobody except Mohammed and two of his sons, Hassan and his wife, daughter, and new baby, four policemen, a gardener, the gardener's daughter, two gatemen, my bodyguard, and all the friends and relations of the above.

My bodyguard is a sketch out of Damon Runyan, a husky young man with a pistol in his pocket and an irresistible urge to tell me how he catches thieves on campus (he is deputy director of campus security), takes them into the shed under the main gate, and "gives them a good lesson." Also that he runs three miles a day, has a lifesaver's certificate, and is the former Lebanese wrestling and weight-lifting champion. So the other morning I said, "Mohammed, come on, we're going jogging." He dropped out after three laps, gasping for breath. (I lasted four.) He's a bit leechy and overly buddy buddy, but he's basically nice as thugs go and I do feel a little safer having him follow me around wherever I go.

Since I arrived I've crossed back and forth between Baabda, AUB, Broummana, etc. half a dozen times and each time I get a new chance to inspect the damage in another part of town. Yesterday the driver took us past the beach area and the Palestinian camps near the airport, and I almost vomited. For several miles you see nothing but wrecked buildings. Some are just showing a couple of large gashes from where a shell hit them, wrecking one or two rooms; others look OK from a distance till you approach and see that the entire interior has been burned out (phosphorus shells); others (not so many) have been hit from the air by blockbusters and the whole apartment house just collapsed all the way down, and you know that dozens of bodies are still in there under the rubble. The worst area is in the camps near the traffic circle on the way to the airport, which looks like a plaster-and-cement version of a forest after a fire: just a vast wasteland of fragments of walls, obliterated by thousands of exploding shells. The Chamoun Sports stadium, which the PLO used as an ammunition and training center, is horribly wrecked. The Summerland Hotel is a burned hulk. There are huge craters from bombs in the roads. In one we saw children swimming, where a water main had burst; in another place the road was full of sewage water.

The area closer to AUB is untouched, but a lot of well to do people used to live between Ras Beirut and the airport and their apartments have been hit. I've already met half a dozen AUB professors who got bombed out and are looking for a place to stay while they get their place fixed up at the cost of ten or twenty thousand dollars that they don't have.

Despite all the destruction and everyone's disgust at what the Israelis have done—and what we read every day that Begin or Sharon has just said—it's amazing how upbeat the mood is here now, at least among almost all the people I've met. People see the departure of the PLO as a great blessing, and with them the prestige of the armed gangs. The Lebanese Army and police force have at last gotten off their behinds and are progressively taking over more and more of the city, and wherever they go they plant a Lebanese flag, so when you drive around and see so many flags they have the appearance of signs of celebration, which they actually are. The last bastion of the Mourabitoun,[8] who do not give up so easily, is Ras Beirut. We don't have the Lebanese army anywhere near AUB. But we do have the police (what Omar, the driver, calls "Squad 16") and the other day when a local Mourabitoun thug tried to force his way into the hospital emergency room at gun point and was told by the cop he couldn't take a gun inside, he shot the cop in the leg, whereupon another cop plugged him full of lead and the whole neighborhood rejoiced.

My mode of travel is to get Omar to drive—he is an A No. 1 tough guy—with Mohammed the bodyguard along for the ride, nervously fingering the pistol I know he has in his pocket. I feel like the gang leader. On a couple of occasions I have also had Squad 16, following me in a Land Rover. They crash around the streets shouting and waving all the other drivers off the road so that they can keep right behind the car they are escorting. Where they were during the fighting nobody knows.

I went to pay a call on President Sarkis the other day! On Monday I'm going to visit the Prime Minister, Wazzan. After that I expect to visit Bashir Gemayel ("Super Beast," as the foreign journalists call him). He takes office on the 23rd and the country is holding its breath to see how conciliatory to his opponents he's going to be, as well as whether the Israelis decided to give him a chance by getting the hell out of the country. A Syrian plane was shot down here a few days ago. The joke is that whenever a Syrian pilot takes off, they always give him fifty pounds to put in his pocket for the taxi fare home.

It's time to go downstairs and have a quick cup of tea and then to the tennis court to take on Nadim Khalaf. More later. Don't forget to write!

Love,

Dad

P.S. I'm sending this via Paris with Samir Thabet who is leaving for a holiday. John gets the carbon copy.

Marquand House
September 17, 1982
Dear Family,

We've had a couple of exciting days. First I was awakened late at night with a phone call from Radwan Mawlawi, our public relations officer, telling me of Bashir Gemayel's assassination. The bomb had gone off at 4:00 that afternoon and it was widely known, but it had been claimed that he had escaped. But I had been indoors at a meeting and had heard nothing. The next morning there were fusillades of gunfire all over west Beirut (some of which sounded so close I thought it was coming from Nicely Hall, next door—but it wasn't), as the unreconciled diehards in this part of town celebrated the news of the murder. Meanwhile the Israeli air force buzzed the city for over an hour, announcing that they were in charge. Of course people here hardly need to be told that, after the events of the summer, in fact they are so completely convinced of it that they assume the Israelis organized Bashir's assassination, a theory that even I tend more or less to believe. Then, through the day, we began hearing bits of news about the Israeli army moving into the outskirts of West Beirut.

Yesterday morning I awoke to more air force buzzing and to the sounds of artillery and automatic guns firing. Rashid Khalidi phoned from his house near the Patriarchate (half way to Bab Idriss) to say that Israeli tanks were around the corner, and as a Palestinian and PLO enthusiast he wanted refuge in an empty faculty apartment, which we got for him. An AUB campus guard reported the Israelis were at the Riviera Hotel, half a mile up the Corniche beyond the faculty apartments. Finally at 9 A.M. I looked out the window from David Dodge's office on the third floor of College Hall and there on Rue Bliss, just outside Uncle Sam's and Feisal's, were a dozen Israeli infantrymen, armed to the teeth. They carefully peeked around the corner up Rue Jeanne d'Arc to look for snipers and then scampered, one by one, like scared rabbits across the intersection. More soldiers kept coming and doing likewise. Meanwhile an occasional Lebanese civilian would show up and wander casually down the street, oblivious to the war around him, while others watched curiously from balconies. Finally a parade of three or four gigantic tanks rumbled up Rue Bliss. They all proceeded down toward Rue Sadat and up toward the Mayflower Hotel. We heard a great deal of firing, including deafening artillery explosions, all over Ras Beirut, as the Israelis covered themselves before moving in on their targets—buildings where they thought the Mourabitoun or the PPS might be holed up—and didn't bother to see if in fact there was really anybody there. Quite a few buildings in Ras Beirut were heavily damaged and the AUB Hospital has treated perhaps 100 casualties. This morning everything is quiet except for a few isolated explosions. I think the Israelis have not completed their occupation of the Basta area and later this morning (it's now not quite 7 A.M.) we may hear more sounds of battle.

I had it all figured out what I would say if I had to confront the Israeli army at the gates to the campus, but no one came. We gave the staff the day off, a very generous gesture since hardly anyone came anyway. Several secretaries and deans hung around the president's office with me all day watching from the windows. Later, a young man from the U.S. Embassy came up to visit me at Marquand House. He said the Israelis had promised to leave two places untouched: The AUB and the U.S. Embassy. But the Israelis kept asking whether there weren't any terrorists on the campus ("Are you sure there aren't any terrorists?") and finally when they asked whether there might be any terrorists taking refuge in the Embassy, the Americans told them to shut up. But yesterday morning, as the Israelis approached the Embassy area, they fired at a U.S. Marine guard standing on the Embassy roof, narrowly missing him. When it was demanded what the hell they were doing, their commander said, "Oh, well we thought that perhaps the Mourabitoun had taken over our embassy and that he might be a Mourabitoun."

Apparently the Marine guards were just hoping that the Israelis would try to enter the Embassy so they could have an excuse to blast them. I was told that the Marines have watched the bombardment of Beirut all summer from the ambassador's residence and have acquired a thorough dislike of Israel.

Later, after the BBC and breakfast: I've just heard the news that Begin has generously insisted on staying in Beirut to keep order until the Lebanese army in cooperation with him is ready to step in, and that Ghassan Tueni at the UN has called Israel's excuses "ludicrous and revolting." Amen. It really is very sad, for until the assassination it was obvious that the country was moving rapidly toward reconciliation and the army and police were progressively taking over the city without a fight. Even after the assassination, if the Israelis had kept their hands off, the Lebanese could have taken care of themselves. Evidently this is not what Begin wants. We now have to wonder when, if ever, the Lebanese will get their airport back and have a chance to breathe again. Without the airport, no foreign students will be very keen to attend AUB and it will cost us additional millions.

I'm sending xeroxes of this to John, Susie, and Granny, plus copies of the photo of me visiting President Sarkis. Notice the splint on my right finger, the result of catching a tennis ball the wrong way six weeks ago. I'll have to wear it another five weeks. It makes typing a bit difficult, but nothing compared to the difficulty of flossing my teeth. Just try flossing your teeth, especially the lower ones, with your middle finger extended. (That part is for Susie's benefit.)

Much love to you all,
Mac/Dad/Malcolm

Sept 19
Dear Family,

No one has decided to travel yet so I may as well add a bit to my saga. The Israelis have this town buttoned up tight: crossing from or to East Beirut is impossible and tonight there is a curfew. The country has run out of mazout and there is no electricity—except here at AUB where we have our own generator. We too were about to run out of fuel for the generator and had we done so, the hospital would have closed down, pulling the plug on 30 patients on respirators, etc. So guess whom we got 30 tons of fuel from this morning? You guessed it. Yesterday Mohammed, my bodyguard, drove Joe Simaan and me around town in his ancient Fiat looking for Israeli military headquarters, which turned out to be in the Riviera Hotel just down on the corniche. The lobby was full of scruffy looking soldiers lounging around, plus one plump woman of uncertain age and even more uncertain virtue lounging with them. "Does anyone speak English?" I asked. Yes, said a soldier and Yes, said Madame. "We have an emergency. We need fuel oil for our hospital," I said. Madame turned to her companion and said, "They have an emergency. They need fuel oil for their hospital." Presently a bearded officer with thick glasses and a cap, looking exactly like Woody Allen in "Bananas," appeared and introduced himself as Major Spiegel.

Presently Major Spiegel produced Lieutenant Mayer, a young army doctor, and explained that he would inspect our hospital. So he got into a truck with two soldiers and off we went, and the hospital staff looked on wide eyed as they walked around the corridors and saw the X ray room, a lab, etc. Fortunately we kept him out of the wards. He left, and an hour later I was summoned to meet Colonel Uri Abu Yaakov in the hospital lobby who explained in Arabic that he was in charge of "Social Affairs." "Want to dance?" I almost asked. He asked a few questions, a huge crowd of the curious gathered, and he left as I explained briefly to the crowd that we were desperate for fuel, and they murmured approval.

In any event, this morning they delivered the fuel in two tanker trucks without a hitch and declined to accept payment, nor did they make any effort at publicity. Abu Yaakov said he would return in three days to see what else we needed. (We will probably need more fuel.) It's just as well they didn't charge us, because now I don't need to deduct $1500 for the damage to our gate made by the tank the other day; in fact, to make up the $1500, I figure they still owe us a couple of tons of fuel. I asked Abu Yaakov when they would open the crossings to East Beirut. "It'll be another two or three days," he said, "until we finish cleaning the city of terrorists." This seemed a particularly graceless remark since the Shatila-Sabra massacre had just occurred yesterday, but I smothered my temptation to say anything, especially since Col. Abu Yaakov looks pretty mean.

I don't know what reports you are getting about the massacre but here there is no one who doesn't hold Israel responsible, since they let the Haddad people into the area in the first place and sat by and watched through binoculars as the massacre took place. In the words of a U.S. embassy man who had been down to survey the scene there, they supervised the whole thing. They are now trying to pin it on the Phalanges, their erstwhile friends. More information also continues to come in about their behavior on other fronts, e.g. their irresistible urge to squash cars with their tanks and to trash apartments they are searching. Usama Khalidi is the latest victim of the latter. It's strangely in contrast to their nice handling of the fuel situation and the very mild-mannered young doctor who visited the hospital.

Getting away from such matters, I can report that I've had a constant stream of visitors and that I've been reviewing the household budget with Muhammad Lichtenwalner. It appears that I need about $500 a month for food for myself and my faithful retainers, plus maybe another $100 for the guests that AUB doesn't pay for. Fortunately I don't have a lot of other needs, that is until I start buying things, such as a radio, TV, and exercise bicycle. I am told that swimming at the AUB beach is a sure path to eternal diarrhea, so a bicycle may be better exercise. I can use it in my bedroom while listening to the news.

Also today, after 17 days in this house, I noticed that there were no pictures on any of the walls. So Muhammad and I rummaged around a little and came up with some pictures in the closets and there are now five large Roberts lithographs hanging in the dining room, plus a lovely painting of an old Oriental gentleman smoking an enormous village-style pipe hanging in the living room. I also unearthed an autographed photo of Theodore Roosevelt, inscribed "Best Wishes to Beirut College" dated 1905. I think I'll take it to my office.

Sept 20: Raja Khuri is due back in Beirut, via Jounieh, this afternoon and I expect he will be carrying a bag full of mail, the first letters I will have gotten from any of you except Susie. The only problem is that with the crossings closed, Raja may have to wait in East Beirut for another couple of days. I'm anxious to hear from all of you! For the moment we are really incommunicado: with the electric shortage in Beirut the telephone lines are out, I think the telex is going to be too, and no travelers are getting in or out. Plus there is a curfew from 5 P.M. to 8 A.M. But don't worry: we have plenty of beer and wine in Marquand House and, with our campus generator humming away on its Israeli oil, my air conditioner is working fine here in my study on the second floor, and so is the radio I borrowed from Hassan, on which I get the BBC.

Sept 21: Raja just arrived bearing a huge stack of mail from you. He is coming to have lunch with me imminently and as I have to give this to a traveler I don't even have time to read your letters first.

I just went to the Medical gate to refuse admission to two Israeli generals and seven or eight soldiers. The top general, Ben Gal, was apparently Deputy Chief of Staff and a Harvard graduate, and just wanted to tour around. I told him I too had gone to Harvard and would have liked to escort him on another occasion but that we had strict rules, the situation was sensitive, and his government had assured mine that they wouldn't touch us, etc. He was very nice and apologized for bothering us.

Things are really looking up once more with the election of Gemayel II and the announcement of the return of the Marines.

Love, Dad/Malcolm

Sept 24, 5:45 A.M.
Dear Family,

I woke up early as I often have been doing, and while I am waiting for the BBC at 6:00 I'll send you a few lines. Einar Larson, our Controller, is at last leaving tomorrow for the US. Like many others, he kept waiting for Beirut Airport to open, but it never did and he lost weeks of vacation time. Kamal Salibi is in the same boat: he wants to go to Jordan. Poor Kamal has been very nervous about the Israelis and what they might do to him, since he has many Palestinian friends and has written an article showing that the ancient Hebrews were not in Palestine or Egypt but in what is now Saudi Arabia. I assured him that the Israeli army neither knew nor cared, but he assured me that they know everything.

I went with Raja Khuri and Samia (Mrs Usama) Khalidi and her daughter to see their apartment. It is in a building housing the PLO Research Center, which the Israelis decided to dismantle. A huge truck was parked outside, loaded with office furniture and books and files. Half a dozen soldiers were lounging around outside, looking extremely uncouth and wearing a bizarre assortment of civilian hats which they had stolen from the Khalidi apt. I explained that the apt belongs to our professor and not the PLO and we would like to visit it and discuss the situation with an officer. Several officers eventually came and we went up. The apartment had been totally trashed: furniture, clothes, papers strewn wildly in every direction as if a hurricane had struck the place. The door was smashed in (though Samia had pointedly handed a key to the neighbor in front of an Israeli officer the day they came), a big mirror broken, someone had deliberately missed the toilet by three feet with a large dropping, etc. etc. Strangely and contrary to the rumors spread by neighbors, they had not touched the piano nor the TV set. The officers were clearly very shaken and ashamed, although they said a previous unit (that had first entered the neighborhood) had been responsible. I think their embarrassment made our visit worthwhile. The youngest officer, Lieut. Zeev Ben-Aryeh, aged 20, said before we went up: "You know, we're not saints, and this is war," and later remarked that after being in the field for weeks without a bath or change of clothes and in the presence of a hostile population, nice boys like him found themselves doing surprising things. His father is Dean of Humanities at Hebrew University. He was a nice boy and I'm sure at home he, no more than John, would not go to the bathroom on the floor—not No. 2 anyway.

Equally nice was the Israeli general who wanted to visit the campus the other day. I met him and his half dozen soldiers at the Med. Gate and said no, and they very sweetly said they understood, and went away. We are now eagerly waiting for all the other Israelis to go away too, and especially to leave the airport to its rightful owners. Everyone is delighted that the Western peacekeeping forces are returning, though people take note of the difference between the French and Italians and the American Marines: the former declare that they will fire if fired upon, while the position of the latter is that if there is any shooting they will promptly pull out. There's nobody so tough as the Marines.

I loved the big batch of letters from all of you that Raja brought with him—Ann, boys, Granny, Susie and John. Also the photos and the clippings. I can't figure out why the Dodgers drew such a small crowd the night Steve was pitching, unless it's because he didn't start the game.

I can hear out the window, as I do every morning before breakfast, the plunk of tennis balls from the court down below, and out the window I can see retired professors out for their early morning walk on this campus which doubles as a park for those with access to it. I heard the BBC midway thru the previous page of this letter and will now go down (it's 6:30) and have a quick breakfast before going to the office and trying to phone Pacific Palisades to find out what's going on out there. I'm excited about planning for November–December and seeing all of you, and will be able to anticipate a bit more specifically when I find out about your schedule. At 8:00 I have a visit from David Ignatius of the *Wall Street Journal* (who wrote the article in June about AUB, "Guerrilla U."), at 9:00 from a real estate agent who wants to lease and develop the OPD site, etc. etc. And I have to see what's on the telex from NY. Then I'll get this letter xeroxed and address it to each of you and give the envelopes to Einar Larson. I also have to get someone to get some cash for me to give the servants as a holiday bonus.

Lots of love to each of you,

Dad/Malcolm

PS: An hour later in the office: I've been trying for the last 15 minutes to dial your number, Ann and boys, but I keep getting a busy signal. Either international lines are tied up or Steve is talking to some cute cheerleader. Now I have one of the secretaries dialing for me so I can attend to some truly presidential duties, like writing this.

Just as I was leaving Marquand House to come here with Muhammad my bodyguard, we had a telephone message from the International College gate that the Israeli army was demanding admission to the campus. So Muhammad and I scooted right over there and I had a very angry conversation in Arabic with a young Israeli, telling him that it was they who are the "mukharribeen" (terrorists, more accurately wreckers) here and it was none of their business what went on in Beirut among the Lebanese and Palestinians, that it was they who had wrecked this city and killed 20,000 people this summer, and that this was an American school etc. etc. I never would have planned to talk like that because it could have proved overly provocative, but after all the previous calm and polite conversations I have had with these people over the past week, plus the horrible visit to Usama's apartment yesterday, I felt really angry. Since the Israeli army is now evacuating West Beirut and should be out in another day or two, it seems as if they just have an uncontrollable itch to carry out a few last minute bashes before they have to leave. Anyhow, I guess my anger paid off, for the Israelis left with their tails between their legs and the crowd of onlookers seemed very pleased and proud to hear someone telling them to go to hell.

Later: I've just talked to Ann and Steve, and now it's time to get to work. Yousef Ayoub is coming by to tell me something. Did I tell you Ann, that they had me for dinner soon after I arrived? You would have been richer if you had married him, but I'm better looking and even more cultivated.

Love, M.

Sept 30
Dear Family,

This is a day to celebrate. First, I finally reached Najeeb Halaby by phone after trying for days, and I learned that we will indeed change the Trustees meeting to December 10 and 11. This means that I can be home for Christmas!! Secondly, Beirut Airport opened today and it was music to everyone's ears, including mine, to hear the shrill sound of planes flying low over the campus after all the eerie silence for the past months.

A CBS camera crew came to Marquand House and filmed an interview with me about the life of the American community in Beirut. You can tune in to the "Sunday Morning" show on October 10 and have a look at me!

I went this morning to pay a courtesy call on Pierre Gemayel at his office in downtown Beirut. He was very courteous but looked 100 years old and delivered an unnecessarily strong message of complaint that AUB neglects Lebanon and runs after the Arabs. I tried to reassure him. They say he aged a lot when Bashir was assassinated. I hope to meet Amin (the Pres.) soon. Every time I go anywhere I have a fresh look at the destruction of this city. Some streets, wrecked in 1976, now have thick growths of bushes and even trees filling them. Rubble is everywhere. The Lebanese army has wreaked the latest bit of destruction, albeit in a necessary cause: they bulldozed the shacks erected by squatters at Pigeon Rocks and near San Simon Beach, but now someone will have to cart that much more wreckage away. In addition to the wreckage there is the garbage, of which there are mountains. In East Beirut most neighborhoods look like paradise: clean, tidy, and normal. West Beirut is a hell hole. But then the AUB campus is a cocoon of spectacularly lovely trees, flowers, and buildings.

Another plane is just flying over. More happy people.

I'll be sorry to miss the Middle East Studies Association meeting in Philadelphia the first week of November, and much sorrier not to see any of you till a whole month later. But the thought of being in Pacific Palisades for Christmas is more appealing than I can say, and I wouldn't miss the chance for anything. Hopefully I'll get there in time to catch a few of Steve's basketball games and watch Andrew wash the cars.

It's now half an hour later and I am in my upstairs study at Marquand House. My gippy tummy has returned so I can't look forward to a good dinner, not to mention a beer beforehand. Mohammed keeps very meticulous track of all the food consumed around here. The other night I had four friends for dinner and the next day he showed me a list of what was consumed and what it cost, totaling LL. 189 ($40). He writes everything in English, but in Arabic script, and it was only with great effort that I was able to make out unfamiliar words that turned out to be "meat," "fejtibil," "wal nuts," "soub," etc. So I told him it would be easier if he would just write the Arabic words. I'm sending it to Susie.

I am enclosing some press interviews that appeared here and that I liked—especially the one that referred to meeting me in my "immense office." (It really is!) I hear I also made the front page of the *Herald Tribune* for chasing Israeli soldiers away from the IC gate. But that's nothing, compared to getting to pitch in Dodger Stadium, or to be the leader of a whole Boy Scout troop at Catalina Island.

Much love to each of you,

Dad/Malcolm

Marquand House

October 5, 6:30 A.M.

Dear Family,

Yesterday I got a batch of mail brought by Terry Prothro, containing a heap of AUB business mail, a letter of Susie's dated Sept. 26, and letters from Ann and John that were more than a month old. Someone else must have picked up the rest of my mail from NY, but where are they? I did love the letters I got, despite their old age, and I do hope that before another month passes you'll all write to me again!

I went to Ainab over Saturday night to stay with the Kennedys in the former Kerr house. Ainab was lovely, nothing to disturb the peace and quiet except a thousand bird hunters whom the Israelis forgot to disarm. The Israelis have all left the area and we went for a sunset walk on the Gunroad. Ted built a fire in the living room after dinner and we had a cozy evening reading the newspapers under various dim lights, just like the old days, except that every time the fire began to look promising, Ted jumped up and poured a little water on it. His idea of keeping it under control prevented it from amounting to much, but the next morning he proudly announced that it still had live sparks in it.

I have had some interesting visits recently. Last week I went to see Pierre Gemayel and Saeb Salaam, the Minister of Finance, and Charles Malik. I hope to visit the new President of the Republic soon. Gemayel looked old and drawn, and treated me to a long lecture in French about how AUB has always turned its back on Lebanon and chased after the Arabs. Salaam I found fascinating and attractive in every way, and I can see why people say that he has done more than anyone to hold this country together. Dr. Malik was fine and we had an interesting discussion about AUB's poor relationship with the Maronites (I told him what Pierre Gemayel had said), but toward the end he began preaching about how only the Christians are capable of anything worthwhile and I felt irritated. But he and Mrs. M. were very friendly and asked repeatedly about Mother. Every time I've talked to Mrs. Malik for the past twenty years she has always begun by saying that the last time she saw me I was only four years old.

Salwa Es-Said invited me to lunch on Sunday (just following my return from Ainab), along with the daughter of Munib Shahid (friend of Granny and Grandpa), the Minister of Finance, and the Pres. of the Lebanese University, which Phyllis Salem always likes to call Leb U. (Usama Khalidi calls Damascus University Dam U.) The Prime Minister was also supposed to come but cancelled at the last minute! I also attended a lunch the other day at the Bristol to which the Minister of Information invited me. So I'm having some fancy social life. What has been much more fun however has been the visit to the Kennedys in Ainab, etc.

Last night Terry and Najla Prothro came and had dinner with me and we had a long discussion about what to do about

David Dodge. John Cooley who came to lunch also has some ideas, and he and I are going to visit Dillon this afternoon to explore them. I am thinking of making a trip to Damascus to work on the matter.

The work schedule is just now about to become very heavy. A sign is the heap of mail from the NY office that Terry Prothro brought me, concerning the budget and other such fascinating matters. The campus is now suddenly full of students getting ready to sign up for classes. My bodyguard Mohammed continues to live at Marquand House and follow me everywhere. He even rode up to Ainab and back, in my gleaming white Buick limousine driven by Omar. (One of these days I'm going to get to drive it myself.) But now I find that he is putting in for a fortune in overtime pay, so I think I'd better cut down on his involvement.

I have a busy day coming up. My first order of business now is to go downstairs, have breakfast, and check with Mohammed about the money that is owed to him on David Dodge's account: old bills from Smith's that he has to pay, etc.

Much love to each of you,
Malcolm

Princeton, New Jersey
October 8, 1982
Dear Malcolm,

I wanted to send you a telex or a cable or any message that would arrive on your birthday carrying my love and faith and best wishes to you in whatever you are doing, for I know you will give it your best. But there must be something you need that you can buy in Beirut and charge $25 to me to be paid by me as soon as I next see you! I hope you will be surrounded by good friends and though no one can replace your own very special family with all their love, art, imagination, great humor and wildly expressed ideas—still there are with you the same faithful, happy, loveable good friends you've known for years and years who will help you through this year.

I've loved getting my copy of your family letter. I feel I'm there hearing about all that goes on each day. I hope Usama is recuperating fast. Give him my best.

I hope nothing prevents your inauguration ceremony on Dec 3rd. How I wish I were 75 and could be there! Instead, I can't forget that I'm almost 87, and have to depend on my imagination and pride and love for you. I wish Dad were here in person. Nothing could please him more than to see you made President of A.U.B. which he loved so much and to which he gave his best.

I hope by December the cataract operation on my good eye will produce good results. If you can go to your family in California for Xmas, I'd love to go too, even if my arthritis goes with me. Susie and John and Nancy have all written and perhaps will come for Thanksgiving.

I think and pray for you (and for David's safe return) every day. May God bless you and keep you and give you an abundance of his Wisdom and Love.

As always,

Your loving Mother

October 11, 1982

Dear Family,

We have had some exciting things happen in the past few days. On Friday we learned that Elie Salem had been appointed Foreign Minister and Deputy Prime Minister, totally without warning. Not bad for an AUB Dean of Arts and Sciences! Everybody at AUB is thrilled, the more so as at the same time Dr Adnan Mrouweh, Prof of Obstetrics, was made Minister of Health, Labor, and Social Affairs. I for one think it only appropriate that an obstetrician should be in charge of Labor. Yesterday I went up to Baabda for lunch with Elie and Phyllis, who were besieged by well wishers, relatives, etc. They are obviously extremely pleased. Elie is leaving here on Sunday with President Gemayel for a whirlwind trip to the U.S.—the UN, the White House—and back via Paris and Rome. So he is in for an exciting time.

The same day I went to the Bristol Hotel where Hassan Saab had invited me to lunch. It turned out to be a fancy gathering in a private dining room—various ambassadors, a former prime minister, etc.—and I was startled and very touched when Hassan, who had somehow learned that it was my birthday, produced a cake and the assemblage of Lebanese dignitaries attempted to break into song. So I managed to come up with a little speech telling Hassan that I had come back to Beirut because of people like him. I seem to be his only fan, but I find him very loveable. Then that evening, while I was having dinner with Al Reynolds (Head of International College) and wife, my household retinue of cook, waiter, and bodyguard appeared on the doorstep each with what looked like a glass of scotch and proposed a sort of toast to me. They each also gave me a present, which greatly embarrassed me, especially as I had not intended to mention to anyone that it was my birthday. At least the spilling of this news earned me a peck on the cheek from Mrs. Reynolds, which I told her I badly needed. Only Elie and Phyllis and Ali Ghandour have kissed me lately.

Today some really big stuff happened, at least it might turn out to be. I have been talking up a plan for a closed-doors seminar in late November of around 15 AUB alumni and friends to discuss the future of AUB's role in Lebanon, including how it can pave the way for raising money, pleasing the government, and getting the alumni to contribute. Well, today I hit the jackpot when I was invited to lunch with Rafik Hariri by one of his chief assistants, a banker who is an AUB alum named Hajj. Rafik Hariri, if you don't know, is a Lebanese billionaire from Sidon who started out poor and ill-educated until he struck it rich in Saudi Arabia as a partner of King Fahd. He is a most unusual man who has been giving away hundreds of millions of dollars over the past few years in Lebanon. He built a huge super-modern hospital near Sidon and hired the AUB to run it (this will start in a few months but won't bring us much money) and now has assigned his construction company and its fleet of hundreds of huge trucks to collect all the trash in Beirut, Sidon, and Tyre at a cost of something like $15 million. All at once in the past couple of weeks Beirut has been transformed from a garbage-ridden pile of bombed-out rubble to a spotless, appealing, almost nostalgic pile of bombed-out rubble. In short, it looks like the good old days. Hariri, who is only 38 years old, loves to do things for the public without publicity or gain of any kind.

In any event, it now looks to me as if Hariri might wind up coming to AUB's rescue in a big way. First he asked what besides his hospital AUB might like to collaborate in, and I suggested he should just attend our seminar to help us decide how AUB could "serve Lebanon" and he agreed on the spot to attend. Since he lives in Riadh and spends lots of time in Paris I never thought he would want to come, but he said that since he has his own plane he didn't see why not. His mere appearance at the seminar will amount to a tremendous endorsement for us—all the others will get the electrifying message that Mr. Moneybags is on our side— and since the central message to the gathering will be that we need money, I feel sure he will give us some substantial help.

Antoine H. came to dinner tonight. He is such a shadowy fig- ure, no one knows what he does. He does spend some time being chairman of the board of the school founded by his father. Five years ago I spent three days with him in the Abu Dhabi Hilton without learning what he was doing there. My theory is that he either sells arms or sells Kleenex.

Much love to you all,
Dad/Malcolm

October 18, 1982
Dear Family,

I have stayed home to nurse my gippy tummy and write the speech I have to give to the students at Convocation (first day of classes) this Thursday morning. The speech is mostly a veiled justification of raising tuition 30% and warning the students against political activities, so I am feeling like a bit of a Fascist at the moment. It will be fun to put on my bright new yellow and black Johns Hopkins doctoral costume with the floppy hat, looking like the newest canary in the AUB cage, and get up there and tell the students where it's at. I wonder if any of them will be listening.

We watched Amin Gemayel's speech to the UN live on TV this afternoon, and saw Elie Salem conspicuously in the background. Everyone is very excited that our Dean of Arts and Sciences is now Foreign Minister and hob nobbing with Reagan, the Pope, and such. I haven't met any more bigwigs recently, not since having lunch a week ago with Rafiq Hariri, hero of Beirut garbage collection. But at least I can say I know Elie!

I played tennis early this morning, again with Samir Deeb, a biology professor. My other partners include Nadim Khalaf, Munir the trainer, and occasionally a gatekeeper named Mohammed who at the age of 50 or more likes to walk from Beirut to Nabatiya (50–60 miles). He drops in at Marquand House often for a cup of tea with the servants in the kitchen, and Mohammed the cook always refers to him as "Single-Hajj." This is to distinguish him from "Triple Hajj," Omar the head of the motor pool, who has made the pilgrimage no less than three times.

The office work has become extremely busy now that everyone is back and the school year is getting under way. I love it! There is lots of wheeling and dealing to be done with our $58 million budget, which would be $80 million if we were doing all the things we should be doing.

Did I tell you I met Thomas Friedman of the *NY Times,* a very attractive fellow. Also other journalists from time to time. Next week, Oct. 27th, I am going to Zgharta near Tripoli to meet former President Frangieh, who is close to the Syrian regime and may have some way of helping obtain David Dodge's release.

Later, in the office: someone is going to carry this to the U.S. so I'll finish it up. I've spent half the day (or so it seems) signing my name blindly to forms and letters thrust before me. Wherever I see the word "President" I automatically write my name. Then I notice that what I am signing are form letters to people full of

Lebanese English, like "I wish you all the success." By the time I'm through here, I'll be speaking that way too.

Love to everybody,

Malcolm/Dad

November 6, 1982

Dearest Ann,

It's my usual letter-writing time: 6:30 A.M. Actually I've been up for an hour and have replied to a letter from an old ACS friend, Lois Glessner, whom I had not seen for thirty years. She saw a notice about me and wrote. As her envelope was labeled "Girl Scouts of Greater Philadelphia," I was a little slow to open it at first.

Yesterday I finally paid a courtesy call, with Samir Thabet, on President Gemayel. He gave us a stern lecture about AUB as a hotbed of violence and subversion, and said it had been an "intellectual base for terrorism." It was clear that he had thought up this message carefully in advance. I did not appreciate it at all, especially since, whatever our shortcomings in the past, we have gone to such lengths of late to put AUB back together as a nonpolitical institution. It seemed to me that he had been talking to his father, who gave me a similar lecture a month ago.

The previous day I finally made it to Zgharta to visit President Frangieh, together with Elias Saab who had been his Minister of Finance and, I gather, is still looking after his finances. It was a sparkling day—we have had many lately—with the sea as calm as glass, and a gorgeous drive up the coast to Tripoli. It is a bit of a shock to find how close the Syrian Army still is to Beirut, for shortly after Jubail you pass into their territory at a check point and realize that all at once you are in somebody else's turf. But there were no incidents, and by prearrangement we were met at the check point by an escort vehicle sent by Frangieh, which led us for the remaining hour's drive up past the cement works at Shekka that pollute the atmosphere, past the salt-drying basins, through a small corner of the city of Tripoli, and then inland across the hills to Zgharta, now a good sized town. Frangieh lives in a palatial estate that he probably robbed the country half blind in order to pay for, but maybe he wanted to be sure that his palace was even grander than Chamoun's, down near Damour, which the PLO destroyed in 1976.

Elias and I spent an hour alone with Frangieh discussing David's whereabouts, then were invited for lunch with an intimate circle of fifteen of his closest retainers. (I was told later that it was an unusually small crowd that day.) Frangieh sat in the middle and held court, with the rest of us seated around a very long table in a very ornate and regal dining room. He consumed a large glass of Scotch on the rocks with his lunch. His son and daughter, in their 30s, were there, both being AUB graduates; his son runs the militia and seemed like a rather unpleasant young man, but I liked the daughter, who lived in the Hostel as a freshman the year you were there and who remembered Mother very well.

Frangieh was actually a very attractive character, in his mid 70s, full of humor and eager to reminisce about all sorts of things. He speaks no English so I cranked up my Arabic for the occasion. Actually I am using Arabic more here than I did in Cairo, and I think I am making some progress with it. The Egyptian elements in it washed out a long time ago, probably with my first glass of Arak. Frangieh has a reputation as a country bumpkin and a gang leader. According to Adnan Iskandar, he was once presented with a bullet proof limousine, and it was explained to him that bullets fired at the car could not penetrate the glass. "Never mind," he said, "if there's going to be any shooting it's going to be from the inside out." He seemed a bit more refined than this to me.

As you can see from the enclosed copy of my letter to Doris Dodge, his message about David was not very encouraging. I am now beginning to fear for the first time that his captors may have disposed of him and have been deliberately spreading rumors of various sorts in order to create a cloud of dust and cover their tracks. It's eerie and ominous. I don't mean that Frangieh is in any way a party to this but he may be hopelessly manipulated by the Syrians. As someone pointed out yesterday, if David were indeed being held in some basement in Beirut, by now someone would have leaked the news, in hopes of gaining a reward.

It's getting near time for breakfast and getting to the office, where I have a full schedule of Saturday morning activities. I must get this letter down to the faculty apartments to give to Harout Armenian who is leaving for the U.S. this morning.

The weather is fantastic: clear, sunny, and getting to be just a little crisp. I went for a lovely walk above Ainab last Sunday, marred only by the sounds of gunfire from Souk El Gharb, where the Kataeb and the Joumblattis have been having it out lately. I may find a way to go on another drive someplace this weekend in the mountains.

Much love always,

M.

.   .   .

Thus within two months of his arrival in Beirut, the parameters of Dad's new life as president of AUB were clearly set out. Against the backdrop of the Israeli occupation of Beirut and the south of Lebanon and the presence of the Syrian army to the east and north, smaller wars continued to absorb Druze, Christian, and other militias. Palestinian civilians, those in refugee camps and successful professionals alike, now lacked the protection of the PLO and found themselves at the mercy of those in charge.

Dad's job was to steer Lebanon's principal university on a steady course, raising desperately needed funds, establishing good relations with the country's political leadership, and attracting students from all quarters. Always, there was room for improvement: money was perpetually in short supply, students now came more from Lebanon and less from throughout and beyond the Middle East as before, and the country's new Maronite president, Amin Gemayel, could hardly conceal his antipathy for AUB generally and Dad personally. Gemayel refused work permits for Dad's new appointees, and dispensed with the customary Lebanese gesture of hospitality—the serving of tea—when Dad paid his courtesy call and received Gemayel's lecture on AUB's role as an intellectual base for terrorism.

Dad was enough of a realist not to be deterred by such challenges and setbacks, and enough of an idealist to persist in working for what he and his colleagues at AUB regarded as the best form of American presence in Lebanon. David Dodge would voice this common conviction at Dad's memorial service a year later: "Malcolm believed in AUB's traditional goals and believed that those goals are relevant in present-day Lebanon and the Middle East. He believed that there is no better American presence in the Middle East than the university." Those goals were the humanitarian ones of goodwill and mutual understanding, fostered through a system of education.

With his family, and particularly my mother, so far away, and with communication under constant strain, Dad knew he had to put the best face on things so that we wouldn't worry too much. But underneath, as becomes clearer through his letters as the year went on, was a fundamental awareness of the gravity of the predicament of AUB and everyone working for it.

During the spring of 1983, a series of bombs exploded in Beirut, marking an ominous downward turn. On February 5 a huge car bomb killed among others the twelve-year-old son of an AUB professor and wrecked once and for all the ill-fated apartment of Usama Khalidi and his family, who finally moved into the vacant house of David Dodge, still missing.

On April 18 a massive truck bomb exploded in the lobby of the U.S. Embassy, causing it to collapse on itself and everyone inside. Hundreds of Lebanese, and dozens of Americans, were killed or injured. Many of those who survived the explosion found themselves embedded with literally hundreds of tiny shards, or filaments, of glass that, little by little, over decades, would push painfully out of the human flesh in which they had been trapped, so that their victims could never put out of their minds what had happened on that day.

Mary Lee MacIntyre, an English teacher at AUB whose husband ran the U.S. Agency for International Development program in Lebanon, had dashed over to the embassy on her lunch hour to do some photocopying, arriving just in time to be caught in the explosion that left her injured and widowed. Rayford Bryers was blown out of a window and landed impaled through the eye on the spokes of the embassy fence, and survived.

Charles Light, a marine guard crushed by concrete and riddled with glass, watched as the eyes of a man trapped in a burning vehicle popped out as he was incinerated, and then, the ending of the man's agony when his best friend took a pistol and shot him dead. Ambassador Robert Dillon was among those who survived and walked out on his own two legs.

Of the American survivors, we have on record the graphic testimony of their own suffering and the suffering they witnessed, due to the case they brought jointly under the Antiterrorism Act, known as *Dammarell v. the Islamic Republic of Iran*. Of the Lebanese survivors we have no such record because for them there has been no provision for testimony or justice of any kind: no lawsuit, no truth commission, no international war crimes tribunal.

"All my brave words sound hollow," Dad wrote to us that spring. He canceled a trip home in early May, since it would "look very casual and cavalier to skip town" at such a time. I heard the news of the embassy explosion on a radio in Harvard Square as my new fiancé and I walked out of a movie theater where, ironically, we'd just seen *The Year of Living Dangerously*. Hans and I began to reconsider the wisdom of our plans for a Beirut wedding that summer.

Dad wrote nothing that spring of the newly radicalized Lebanese Shi'ites, or of the "Islamic Jihad" organization that apparently claimed responsibility for the embassy bombing. Looking only at his letters, one might come to the conclusion that he was unaware of the seriousness of the role of Lebanon's Iranian-supported Shi'ite community.

However, a series of telex communications between the U.S. Embassy in Beirut and the State Department in Washington concerning the "Dodge Kidnapping" shows that in fact Dad had intimate knowledge of Iranian-sponsored activities in Lebanon, and of the role of a certain "Musawi"—a common Shi'ite name—in Baalbek.

The telexes began on January 26, 1983, reporting on "conversations with Kerr" regarding anonymous telephone calls to AUB about the welfare of David Dodge. Exactly when such reporting began is unclear because, like everyone else in Beirut, the embassy had problems with its lines of communication, and it is noted that two reports of conversations with Kerr failed to reach their destination.[9]

Nevertheless, the main body of communications dates from mid-May, when Secretary of State Shultz telexed Ambassador Dillon in Beirut and alerted him to rumors that "AUB President Malcolm Kerr has been getting periodic reports from various student groups that Dodge is alive and no longer 'there' (assumption is 'there' means Bekaa), and that 'further attempts to find Dodge will be dangerous.'" Shultz goes on, "Kerr apparently believes Dodge is held either in Iran or Syria."[10]

Dillon reacted to Shultz's telex immediately, reporting back, "We spoke to Malcolm Kerr May 17. He said he had received report on the whereabouts of David Dodge. About one month ago he heard a report which was so speculative that he decided not to pass it on. The source was [BLANK] who works with AUB on a part-time basis. [BLANK] claims acquaintance with Musawi and associates of Musawi. One of these associates reportedly told [BLANK] that Musawi had indicated that David Dodge's friends would do Dodge a favor by not pressing for info on his whereabouts. [BLANK] said he would report further to Kerr after visiting [BLANK] but he has never been back to see Kerr."[11]

It is not certain how many individuals were referred to by "BLANK" or whether the BLANK in subsequent telexes represented the same or new individuals.

What is clear is that AUB became a natural focal point for negotiating Dodge's release, on the basis of the presence in its student body of family members of those close to the faction involved in the kidnapping.

On June 15, Dad informed the embassy of his "latest conversation [with BLANK.]" He had handed BLANK a letter from David Dodge's wife, and BLANK had told Dad that he had taken the British journalist David Hurst to meet Musawi, who had denied any knowledge of the Dodge affair. BLANK planned to go to Baalbek the following week to meet Musawi again. The embassy official who composed the telex, Robert Pugh, noted that "[BLANK] is on close personal terms with the Libyan ambassador, Druki, in Damascus and visited him recently, asking for information about David and particularly urging that he see that David's captors allow him to send a communication. Druki promised to investigate and to reply by around June 26, when [BLANK] expects to be in Damascus for another visit."[12]

A week later, on June 22, BLANK phoned the AUB communications director and informed him that he had been in Iran, where he had discussed the Dodge affair with senior Iranian officials. On the basis of that discussion, BLANK surmised that Dodge was well.

It was clear by now that negotiations for Dodge's release were possible. BLANK didn't want to be involved in them, and Dad was worried because BLANK had indicated that the Iranians would like, in return for Dodge, their missing charge d'affairs, Muhsin Musawi (indeed another "Musawi"), whom Dad feared was dead.

The next day's telex from Beirut reported that Dad had been unable to get a meeting with BLANK, who was in the southern coastal city of Tyre, and there was no means of direct communication with BLANK. The possibility of using BLANK's family members at AUB as emissaries was raised. Meanwhile, Dad discussed with embassy personnel his intentions for the prospective meeting: he wanted first to "extract as much information as possible [from BLANK]," and then to formulate "a message which AUB would ask [BLANK] to pass to the Iranians."[13] But apparently the meeting still did not happen.

The final telex reporting on Dad's strenuous endeavor to meet with BLANK is dated July 10—two days before he flew home to walk me down the aisle at my wedding on July 16. He was the last one to arrive home for the occasion, and little did I know what was on his mind.

A week later, on July 19, our telephone rang in Los Angeles, bearing incredible news: David had been released in Damascus in a move facilitated by Syria, and was on his way back to his family in the United States.

.   .   .

So Dad knew more than a little of what he was up against. I said good-bye to him for the last time a week after my wedding, where he'd disagreed with the minister about the appropriate moment in the ceremony to give me away. I can still feel his final embrace and remember thinking, "Maybe this won't be the last time, after all."

He headed back to Beirut, this time taking with him my mother and Andrew, as well as Steve, whose otherwise happy visit to Lebanon in advance of his freshman year at the University of Arizona was marred by what the locals called "shelly weather." Exploding shells at the airport, where Steve was waiting to board a plane, meant instead a circuitous journey by car with Haj Omar, over the mountains to Damascus and then on to Amman, where at last he caught a flight back to the United States. Hans, John, and I collected Steve at the airport in Los Angeles in the middle of the night. In high spirits that I now recognize as giddy relief, we cooked up a midnight feast of French toast as soon as we arrived home, and I remember trying to think of Steve's impromptu change of itinerary as just "one of those things."

During Dad's first year in Beirut he had needed for everyone's sake to be as encouraging and positive as possible. As he began his second year, David Dodge was safely home, but there was no joy because now he had his own family's safety to worry about. Shortly after Steve's aborted departure from Beirut Airport, my mother and Andrew fled to Amman by car with Haj Omar and then took a plane to Cairo. There they met up with John, who had just started working for Catholic Relief Services. They returned to Beirut after an absence of six weeks, in time for Andrew to befriend the U.S. Marines who liked to play basketball on the AUB campus. On October 28, the marine barracks were blown up by a suicide truck bomb, and they stopped coming.

With my mother and Andrew in Beirut, Dad didn't write quite as often—though when he did he was more frank. "Poor AUB and Lebanon," he wrote to me on November 19 from the Roosevelt Hotel on his last trip to New York. "I don't know how long we can stick it out." He telephoned me, too, from New York, our last conversation, full of worry for my mother and Andrew, who had stayed in Beirut that week, and pondering the idea that to complete no more than the rest of that academic year might be a wise idea.

He was shot at point blank range at about ten minutes past nine on Wednesday, January 18, on a typically busy morning when he had already been to the bank and paid a visit to the director of the AUB Museum. Later that week when Hans and I had joined the mourners in Beirut, the museum director most willingly agreed to let us have one of the museum's Roman capitals to mark Dad's grave next to the banyan tree outside his office in College Hall.

Later that day, while my mother and Andrew lay down on a bed upstairs at Marquand House trying to get through on the telephone to John in Cairo, Steve in Arizona, and me in Taiwan, a caller came to the house bearing Dad's briefcase. It was fifteen-year-old Andrew, now my mother's protector, who alone received it and cleaned off the blood and tissue to shield her from the sight. A few days later another caller came, this time bearing a small manila envelope with the words "Dr. Kerr's Glasses" typed across it. Now there were four of us to receive the parcel in my mother's stead, and the residue of dried blood in the broken frames was visible only if one looked closely. Why couldn't the glasses have been delivered first and the briefcase second?

In Princeton, where my grandmother had suffered a stroke several hours before Dad fell to the ground, her surviving children gathered to break the news to her. She didn't speak or show emotion, and no one knew how much she'd understood of what had been said to her. Some weeks later she said, "If I start to cry, I'm afraid I'll break."

Directly following the assassination, the U.S. Middle East envoy Donald Rumsfeld flew from Israel to Beirut, where for five hours he met with President Amin Gemayel. Presumably Gemayel served tea. Then Rumsfeld flew on to Paris, where the next day he met with French foreign minister Claude Cheysson, who animatedly declared that there was logic in the marking of AUB as a cultural target, and that this act signaled a new era in anti-Western terrorism.[14]

In Beirut, where the weekly news magazine *Monday Morning* published a cartoon dubbing Dad "The American Victim of Beirut," the new American ambassador, Reginald Bartholomew, began investigating the main suspects. A shrewd man who nineteen years later stated that he still had "every interest in being able to nail the individuals that did this," he could find no evidence of Christian responsibility for the assassination—though in the rumor mill of West Beirut, it was the Maronite Christians with their unconcealed antipathy for Dad and AUB who were regarded as the most likely suspects.[15]

Bartholomew's investigations led instead to the senior Hizballah figure of Hussein Musawi. So many years later, when I heard Bartholomew describe Musawi's denial of responsibility, I recalled the denial Musawi had issued a couple of months before Dad's assassination, in answer to a question by then Associated Press reporter Terry Anderson about the suicide bombing of the marine barracks. Musawi had denied responsibility for the attack on the marines, though he expressed his wish that the opposite were true. Then he had said, "Definitely there will be new operations against them. I hope to participate in future operations."[16] In his video deposition for our trial, Bartholomew stated simply, "If Musawi publicly confesses that he is the one who did it, and he is Musawi operating out of the Bek'aa, *quod est demonstratum* in terms of Syrian responsibility, and Syria then cracks down on them. So Musawi is going to shut up in this sort of a situation."[17]

The police completed their investigation with remarkable speed. After interviewing Dad's secretary, who had seen the killer with his arm outstretched standing behind Dad; a student who had seen two unfamiliar men enter the elevator with Dad; another who saw two unfamiliar men come running down the stairs a few minutes later; a newspaper vendor who saw two men running out of the Feisal's Gate; and the head of AUB campus security who'd found nothing amiss that day, the police filed their thirteen-page report on the day after Dad's memorial service, case closed. They had arrived "immediately" at the scene, where they carefully measured out the patch of dried blood marking the spot where Dad fell, but neglected to determine exactly how many shots had been fired—a matter difficult to resolve since the coroner's report went missing somewhere along the line.[18]

In Washington, two days after the police report was filed, a "Memo suggesting sympathy msg" was received by the National Security Council and acted upon immediately. The final draft of a letter to Mrs. Ann Kerr was ready for President Reagan's signature on February 1, the word "tragic" having been added to "death" and the word "sincere" changed to "heartfelt." A bureaucrat scribbled on the copy of the letter that was filed away in the NSC archives, "Condolence msg sent."[19]

On February 10, the NSC was privy to a State Department memo identifying Hussein Musawi's Hizballah cell as responsible for the murder of

Malcolm Kerr, and after some prodding through the Freedom of Information Act, a copy was dispatched to Mrs. Ann Kerr nineteen years and nine months later.[20]

. . .

What other means had Dad's killers imagined for eliminating him? Had he been better protected, would another scenario have been chosen, necessitating the bringing down of a whole building perhaps, as with the assassination of president-elect Bashir Gemayel in September 1982, or the attempts on U.S. Ambassadors Dillon in April 1983 and Bartholomew in September 1984? If that had happened, might our mother and Andrew have been victims? And if that had been the case and Dad had survived, what would he have done?

If I know nothing else, I know he would have rejected any form of violence. Andrew said this as we prepared for the trial: "While my gut feeling is for revenge, I know that Dad wouldn't want that. In the short time I had him he did teach me the difference between right and wrong."

Why did the perpetrators strike on January 18, 1984? Had they been provoked when on January 11 the sister of Imam Musa Sadr, the founder and spiritual leader of the Shi'ite Amal group who had vanished in Libya six years previously, paid a courtesy call to Dad at Marquand House? With her entourage and my mother sitting nearby, Dad and the imam's sister drank tea together and discussed in Arabic the progress of her son at AUB and the prospects for locating her missing brother. When she'd gone and the news of her visit had spread across campus, Dad looked at my mother and said, "That visit was worth a thousand bodyguards!" Or was it?

Twenty years later, I search through Dad's words, looking as much for the wisdom of someone who spent a lifetime studying the politics of his beloved native land as for the words of a beloved father, to fill in the corners of the story we share so that I can put it to rest and relieve myself of responsibility for the way it ended.

Our quest for legal justice opened a door—forced open a door—I had wanted to keep shut. The remit of our lawsuit, though we demanded its broadest possible terms, still did not provide that concept of "closure" about which one hears sometimes in cases like ours. Instead, many new and important questions were exposed.

Because of who Dad was—a Beiruti by birth and profession—this quest could be accomplished only by looking at the man himself. He was an extraordinary victim of terrorism because he could have helped us to understand, better than almost anyone, what happened to him and why. I have tried to do that without him.

Epilogue

DAD WOULD HAVE ENJOYED making a joke about the fact that the defendant in the case before ours in the upstairs courtroom of the U.S. District Court building in Washington, D.C., was one of the world's biggest multinational hamburger chains. Reading the notice pinned to the courtroom door, having gone through the security check at the main entrance and climbed up the marble staircase, I thought, "We've gone this far to join the ranks of fast-food litigation?"

Of the many differences between the hamburger case and ours, the most important was that in ours the defendants' table was empty. Placed around the two tables before the judge, one for the defense and one for the plaintiffs, were huge leather chairs, more luxurious than anything we had at home. With our group so numerous—there were six of us, my father's sister Dorothy having now joined the suit—we soon took to borrowing one of the chairs from the empty table that should have been occupied by a representative from the government of Iran, or at least by its lawyers.

The name of the fast-food franchise on the courtroom door had now been replaced with one that read, *Susan Kerr van de Ven, et al. v. The Islamic Republic of Iran, et al.*—a daunting collection of words that made me want to run and hide. Feeling cowardly, I pointed out to our lawyers that the lead plaintiff was in fact my mother, and the next day the notice was corrected.

Although the defense table was empty, still the act of testifying before Judge Thomas Penfold Jackson, his two young clerks, our extended family, and one or two members of the public was intimidating. My eleven-year-old son Johan, whose middle name is for the grandfather he never knew, sat through every minute of the proceedings, listening to his

146

adored uncles and grandmother tell the story as it had been for them and watching the tears that came every so often. My mother cried only once, not when she described her last sight of Dad, but when she reached the point in the story where she wasn't able to tell Andrew that his father was dead. The radio had done the job.

At times we thought how much easier it was that we had no people to face or to confront in a physical sense, in that courtroom. But looking back, perhaps there was something missing. For the accused and the accuser to look one another in the eye was at the core of the process employed in the Truth and Reconciliation tribunals in South Africa and elsewhere. While we could work as hard as we wanted to learn and study and understand the context in which Dad had been murdered, and to press for the highest standard of evidence in the courtroom, we had no power through the law to bring about any face-to-face meeting.

Although the Iranian government sent no defense team, presumably on grounds of foreign sovereign immunity, it defended itself in a number of trade and commercial cases being tried in Washington courtrooms. One of these was *Foremost-McKesson, Inc. v. Islamic Republic of Iran,* which involved a claim by Foremost—the ice cream chain—over the Iranian government's nationalization of the firm's dairy operations in Iran following the Islamic revolution.[1] Foremost-McKesson wanted its money back, and the Iranian government was spending a good deal defending its position.

In Iran itself, legislation had been enacted to enable civil lawsuits against the U.S. government for acts of terrorism against Iranian citizens, such as the case of the Iranian commercial airliner shot down by the USS *Vincennes.* The principle of the courtroom, rather than the gun, as the appropriate tool for upholding justice was something both countries had sought at some level to promote.

In the Iranian Parliament, as in the U.S. Senate, the subject of financial penalties for state-sponsored terrorism had engaged the attention of legislators and prompted debate.

In spite of having spent years coming to a decision that legal justice was something we wanted to pursue, still we had not reached consensus on whether or not to include punitive damages in our lawsuit. John, Andrew, and I whisperingly debated the issue around the plaintiffs' table literally until the Court Clerk marched into the courtroom with his call of "All Rise!" and it was Andrew's turn to give the final testimony. The three of us concurred that someone had to make a gesture of reconciliation, to draw a line marking the end of a dispute between people. We decided that punitive damages and their repercussions for future generations were inappropriate.

While we had sought views, advice, and information from outside our family on many aspects of the case, the subject of punitive damages was one we hadn't explored with anyone else. Only other plaintiffs in similar cases would have faced the same unusual decision, one inexorably bound up with devastating loss. It was not a topic one could easily bring up. The sums of money attached to punitive damages seemed incomprehensible, and I had found the subject hard to think about.

It came as a surprise to us, at some point after the trial, to learn that we had been the first plaintiffs not to file for punitive damages. I wondered if others had just gone along with them because others had done it and it was too difficult a subject to unravel and consider. Not only had all previous lawsuits included punitive damages, but in every one the judge had made the decision to award them.

In the months following our trial, other lawsuits came to the District Courthouse under the Antiterrorism Act, and in three cases seeking punitive damages the presiding judges ruled against them. This marked a shift in the broad legal discussion about justice for victims of terrorism. Whether or not our own decision not to file for punitive damages was noted by the judges assigned to those later cases, we like to think it was.

Judge Jackson's ruling on our case arrived in the mail two months later, after we had all gone back to our ordinary lives. We exchanged no e-mails or phone calls that day or in the week that followed. Somehow, while he had found in our favor and made predictable compensation awards, which, if ever turned into reality through a legislative funding mechanism, would constitute half-a-dozen generous pensions and a foundation or two, the arrival of his "Order and Judgment" was deeply shocking. It acted as final confirmation that Dad was dead and that nothing could ever bring him back. In that courtroom, with such intense focus on who he was and how he'd lived his life, it was as though we were able, nearly, to conjure him up. There was a sense of elation in being united in this endeavor, although we knew perfectly well that never again would we devote ourselves so completely to collective memories. The full banality of money, about which one sometimes hears in relation to its use as a tool in trying to make up for something lost, came down with a deafening thud.

It was noted in the Order and Judgment that we siblings had not sought any professional counseling in the aftermath of Dad's death. This was a sign, apparently, that we hadn't been as damaged by the experience as we might have been. The final calculations of appropriate compensation were adjusted accordingly.

That judgment was dated February 2003. A month later, the Bush administration, with its so-called Coalition Forces, began its war on Iraq. It ignored the will of the United Nations and then complained when Iraq did not adhere to the Geneva Conventions. Away from the spotlight, the Israeli government stepped up its bulldozing of Palestinian homes and assassinations of Palestinian leaders, and the United States administration turned a blind eye.

Meanwhile the judiciary branch of the U.S. government continued to address quietly the problem of response to terrorism through nonviolent means. It was in the same month that the bombing of Iraq began that the U.S. courts ceased making awards of punitive damages, bringing the American legal code in line with international standards.

·   ·   ·

In December 2006, four years after our trial in the Washington District Courthouse, Saddam Hussein was hanged.

I knew he was a monster, but I hated the enactment of the death penalty.

The event was watched on googlevideo.com and other Web sites by anyone who had access to the Internet and wished to witness an execution. In a commentary published in the British daily the *Independent*, Robert Fisk put into words what I felt: Yes, Saddam Hussein was guilty of unspeakable crimes, but there were others, too, who bore responsibility for the deaths of uncounted numbers of people in Iraq.[2]

He was referring to the governments who had initiated the illegal war against Iraq, based on unfounded claims of links to the September 11 attacks and weapons of mass destruction. Those governments of course were the American and British administrations. By now I had acquired British citizenship and carried what some people in the world would consider to be two infamous passports.

That war had now plunged Iraq into deadly anarchy. My mother's lifelong Iraqi friend Samiya, with whom she'd shared a dormitory room at AUB in 1954, sent out sporadic messages from Baghdad, describing the steady worsening of life there until finally her relatives managed to arrange sanctuary for her in Sweden—the only European country they could find that would give asylum to Iraqi war refugees.

This particular chapter in history, as some saw it, was the latest tragic episode in a long story of colonial, then superpower, erroneous decision making and misuse of power in a region not properly understood. In the chapter that had seen Dad taken from us, the U.S. government, having financed the Israeli military from its F16s to its ration packs, failed to react to the invasion of Lebanon and the prolonged bombing of Beirut in the summer of 1982. A seismic shift had occurred in U.S.-Arab relations, at ground level.

As Dad's AUB friend and fellow trustee Salwa Es-Said had said to him in that July 1982 telex from Beirut, as the rockets flew past at a rate of three per second, "Those of us who have been supporting the U.S. can no longer do so as long as the U.S. government can tolerate such barbarous activities. The hatred that has been generated is going to overflow onto the campus." It did.

When Dad was shot eighteen months later, a group of AUB trustees paid us a condolence visit in the living room at Marquand House. Najeeb Halaby, chairman of the board and the father of Queen Noor of Jordan, put his arms around me and sobbed. Salwa, a lady I had always admired from a distance, threw her thin arms into the air. "Do you know that in my village, sixty people were slaughtered? What are we supposed to do?"

In a sense, the large and obvious share of Iranian responsibility for Dad's death—the financing and arming of Hizballah, and its direct patronage and support for the quest to eliminate him—was the simplest one

AUB trustees on the steps of Marquand House, the
AUB president's campus residence, during the 1982–83
academic year. Salwa Es-Said is in the front row, far left,
Dad is in the second row, far right, and Najeeb Halaby is
standing next to Dad. Two future AUB presidents, Calvin
Plimpton and Fred Herter, are in the back row, second
from left and far right, respectively.

to respond to. What about the share of my own government in refusing to
condemn and disassociate itself from a violent military invasion that did
so much to help set the stage for the deaths and kidnappings of Americans, on account of their nationality?

This question led me to think about the rights and responsibilities
of citizens in a democracy—my democracy: the right to vote for one's

leaders, the right to participate in government, the right to justice and the rule of law. I came to the conviction that I had a responsibility to become an active citizen, rather than one who let the world take shape around me. Engaging in and endeavoring to help shape a piece of legislation was one way of participating in the democratic system and addressing that responsibility.

After the trial, living as I did in Britain, my newfound convictions played themselves out in my adopted country, too. Being an expatriate was something I could no longer justify, and fifteen years on I applied for British citizenship. Even if I giggled to myself when asked to swear allegiance to the Queen, my new rights and responsibilities made a strong impression. For the first time in my life I joined a political party. The Liberal Democrats seemed to stand for the principles I felt so strongly about: internationalism, justice, and the rule of law, and as its then leader Charles Kennedy put it, "intellectual independence and looking out for the Have Nots in society." The Liberal Democrats were the "third" party and the challengers of the status quo. They were also the only major party in Britain to oppose the war in Iraq from its inception.

Soon after acquiring my new citizenship, the Liberal Democrats were looking for candidates to stand in the upcoming local elections. I laughed when the local party agent came calling to ask if I would stand, but Hans convinced me that it would be a good thing for me—and in any case, you don't win the first time, he pointed out.

A few months later I began a new life as an elected representative for my community on the rural council serving the hundred-odd villages that surround the university town of Cambridge. I got a close-up look at the machinations of democracy, where often idealism had to take a back seat to bureaucracy, personality politics, and funding shortages. I saw for myself that public office attracts people for all sorts of reasons, some altruistic ones. A civil servant at one of my training days described democracy as "slow footed, expensive and cumbersome, but the best system anybody has come up with." Battles over any issue bound up in land or ethics were the most hard-fought and illuminated the range of outlooks in the slice of society we collectively represented. Taking a controversial stand at this very local level sometimes seemed as taxing as testifying

With Hans after the trial, San Antonio, Texas, December 2002.

before the court on the subject of my own father's murder, but I found myself compelled to do so.

· · ·

Engaging in the quest for legal justice had answered many questions about the circumstances of Dad's assassination and had a profound impact on the way I now wanted to live my life. And yet I found it as difficult as ever to listen to the news or read the papers where the Middle East was concerned. I caught the big headlines, of course, but usually I let the fine print pass me by.

On February 14, 2005, in my first year as a councillor, I heard on the news that Rafiq Hariri—the man Dad had written so excitedly about for his let's-get-started approach to cleaning up Beirut's wartime rubble, and who eventually went on to become Lebanon's prime minister and a prime mover in rebuilding a new Beirut—had been killed in a massive truck bomb in Beirut. I felt that familiar sickening thud.

After Dad was killed and my mother became a trustee of AUB, she had pointed Hariri out to me at a board meeting in New York one spring, for he, too, had by now become a university trustee. He was quiet and unassuming. I had no stamina for knowing the details of the events that killed him, though like everyone else I could see the writing on the wall.

A few months later came another front-page headline of assassination in Lebanon. This time the victim was Gibran Tueni, a journalist and critic of the Syrian government, which had been implicated in the murder of Hariri. Gibran's father, Ghassan Tueni, was a familiar face from my childhood, one of Dad's respected acquaintances, himself a journalist and public servant who for a time had served as Lebanon's ambassador to the United Nations. It was the photograph of Gibran's university-aged daughter, eyes closed and head resting on her father's coffin, that yanked me in. In the background stood her grandfather, in anguish.

At home, on my council and in my village, the most contentious issue to come to the fore was that of caravan sites for local Gypsy families. No one wanted them, and there was nowhere for them to go. They were the largest minority group in the district, the one with the lowest life expectancy and the most poorly educated. Public meetings over planning permission for new caravan pitches on the edges of villages were standing room only, and though no punches were thrown, the air was often thick with tension. Public opinion was openly antagonistic, and people were not afraid to use inflammatory language. I would often think to myself, "at least there's no bloodshed." Still, the issues were so deeply layered, the emotions so high, and the perceptions so fixed, that it was hard to visualize a solution on the horizon. What I could visualize was a similar situation in a society without law and order, and in which bloodshed might not be so many steps away.

Apart from those occasional horrific headlines out of Lebanon, I let the troubles of the Middle East recede into the background and devoted myself to my responsibilities as a local councillor.

When a new Israeli invasion and bombardment of Lebanon hit the headlines in the summer of 2006, destroying overnight the new infrastructure that Rafiq Hariri's government had overseen, again I avoided knowing the full details and threw myself into the simplest positive associations with Lebanon that I knew. As the bombs dropped, I spent days sewing pillow covers out of the blue and white linen curtains my

Together with Willem, Ann, Johan (on the camel), the camel driver, Hans, and
Derek, on Christmas Day 2006, at the Sakkara Pyramids in Egypt.

mother had made for the Beirut apartment where I was born. I made
hummous and *kibbeh,* dishes my boys had come to love. I rolled dozens
of stuffed vine leaves, a comfortingly time-consuming task taken from
Claudia Roden's *A Book of Middle Eastern Food* that involved the repeated
soaking of the brine-preserved leaves in boiling water, and the rolling
up of each leaf with tiny spoonfuls of uncooked rice mixed with pars-
ley, cinnamon, tomatoes, onion, and mint, then nestling them tightly together in a large pot, covered with lemon juice and olive oil and steamed
long and slow.[3]

I sat with teenage Johan and Derek one evening, rolling the vine leaves
and watching a TV documentary about two other teenage boys, one Israeli
and one Palestinian, and the utterly different worlds they lived in, only
miles apart. The stuffed vine leaves lasted for days and provided physical
comfort as the news from Lebanon grew worse. My governments—the

American and British administrations—did nothing. Tony Blair, known in Britain as Bush's poodle, kept saying that he could see no point in calling for an early cease-fire.

One afternoon on the radio I heard Claudia Roden, of all people, describe how her venture into cookery came about as a result of her exile from Egypt, the land of her childhood, and the need to remember it in a sensual, physical way.

Another Jewish woman who seemed to throw out a lifeline to me that summer was my mother's old friend Chana Arnon, who had coordinated the University of California study abroad program in Jerusalem for many years. Dutch-born, Chana had emigrated to Israel in 1954, at around the same time my mother went to Lebanon for the first time. I had been a guest at her Jerusalem home many times when I taught at St. George's School in the early 1980s. Although I hadn't seen her in twenty-five years, her warm and gentle manner was vivid in my memory.

As I was critical of my governments' actions and policies in the Middle East, Chana had long been critical of the Israeli occupation of Gaza and the West Bank. In response to the erection of the Wall that trapped Palestinians in their West Bank towns, Chana, together with other concerned Israeli women, formed a group called MachsomWatch, the purpose of which was to maintain a physical presence at various checkpoints along the Wall and to help Palestinians negotiate crossings necessary to get to and from places of work, to visit relatives, and carry on with life.

In the middle of the 2006 Lebanon war, Chana wrote to me:

> I consider what we women here in MachsomWatch are doing, to be creating a bridge—although a very tenuous one—of human solidarity on the very basic level of meeting eye to eye. We go out to meet Palestinians at the friction points between their lives and our government's restrictions on them. We hear stories of horror of people whose lives are completely disrupted by the occupation now entering its 40th year. On the other hand, we hear about the mismanagement of the Palestinian governments too. How did the Middle East go so awry? Is it all because of us? The women are trying to swim against the current, but sometimes we discover

that a lot of people here in Israel are on our side and all human feeling is not lost. I thought that the newly elected Israeli gov't would go in the right direction, but now all my hopes are shattered. Lebanon is in ruins and that is bad for the Lebanese, but also for the future of the whole region. One can only guess at the reprisals and counter-reprisals that will ensue in the coming years, when this war will have been forgotten.

Chana's work with MachsomWatch inspired me, but it was her unspoken plea not to form rigid views of "the other side"—another essential ingredient in ending cycles of violence—that caused me to stop and think.

■   ■   ■

By now I knew that this book, which I had written in the months immediately following our trial, was to be published. I had kept a small file of thoughts scribbled down in the intervening two years, ideas I wanted to add and people I wanted to get in touch with to tie up loose strands.

Among them was a student who had been the editor of the AUB yearbook the year Dad was killed. When Hans and I traveled all the way from Taiwan to Beirut in that awful first week, Basil Fuleihan appeared: a lovely, serious, gentle young man with a twinkle in his eye and a direct but unspoken compassion and empathy for what had just happened to us. At the end of that academic year, he unabashedly dedicated the yearbook to Dad, with pages and pages of photographs, affectionately and admiringly presented, and a copy reserved for us, inscribed and signed, "To the Kerr Family, with our deep appreciation and sincere good wishes from the Yearbook Committee. Basil Fuleihan." A small friendship evolved the following year when Basil went to Columbia to begin a Ph.D. in economics, and Hans and I returned to Harvard. Basil would visit Boston from time to time and our paths would cross. Always there was a shy, respectful quality about him, combined with a disarming smile. After graduate school we lost touch, but I read in an AUB Alumni magazine some fifteen or so years later that Basil had become Rafiq Hariri's minister for economic development, having already established an American-based career in academia. Lebanon was a place where people who

Basil Fuleihan, AUB 1984 yearbook editor, at his desk.

had the privilege of education would often devote themselves to public service, and I knew instantly that that had been the case with Basil.

Now I thought I would get in touch again. With the magical tool of the Internet, I typed his name into the Google toolbar and clicked my mouse one time. A split second later Basil's fate was described in a dozen different ways on my computer screen. The "Praying for Basil" Web site described his sedation in a Paris hospital for more than sixty days following the bomb that had killed Rafiq Hariri. Basil had been sitting in the car next to Hariri but, cruelly, had survived the explosion. He was ten years younger than Dad had been, and his tiny children won't have the reservoir of memories that my brothers and I have to draw on. His was the worst-case scenario, the bystander killed in someone else's spectacular assassination, the one who endured unimaginable suffering that his family will have to bear for the rest of their lives.

Responsibility for Basil's murder will be judged by the International Court, because it is bound up in the Hariri case. In April 2006, twelve months after Basil died in Paris, the UN Security Council established a special tribunal for the Hariri assassination, making it clear, as a BBC Beirut correspondent put it, that "the time for impunity in Lebanon is over."[4]

Most of the thousands of killings in Lebanon's layers of war will not have opportunities to go down the road of legal justice. Somehow, people will have to carry on living, even if they have lost not just one person, but sometimes two, three, four, fifty, or even sixty. Some people will stay sane, but some will go crazy.

People react in different ways when someone they love has been intentionally shot, kidnapped, tortured, blown up, or burned to death. A preexisting framework for legal justice must be in place to preempt any inclinations of retribution, and to provide public recognition of wrongdoing.

The cross-national nature of so much political violence coming under the nebulous heading of "terrorism" demands an international legal code to recognize injustice for those left behind, and to break cycles of violence. The Antiterrorism Act is a step in the right direction.

■   ■   ■

On January 18, 1984, a Wednesday, I taught English classes to Taiwanese students and businessmen in downtown Taipei, as I did every day. At the moment Dad fell to the ground in early morning Beirut, I was boarding the number 72 bus to head home to the suburb of Nankang, where Hans and I lived in a tiny house surrounded by papaya trees.

I made a conscious decision not to listen to the radio when I got home. It was the same choice I'd made most days since the bombing of the U.S. Marine barracks in Beirut back in October, when Dad's fate had seemed to be flaunted before our faces.

In the quiet of the late afternoon, I changed out of my work clothes and moved into our small kitchen to prepare the fish I'd bought at the street market near the bus stop. I sliced ginger and green onions, put the rice on to steam, and set the table. Hans wouldn't be home from his desk at the archives until seven, so I had plenty of time to wind down and enjoy getting things ready.

The phone rang at six o'clock. I had given myself an extra two hours before the world changed forever.

Notes

· · ·

Bibliography

· · ·

Index

Notes

1. Breaking Apart

1. Anna Blundy, *Every Time We Say Goodbye: The Story of a Father and a Daughter* (London: Arrow Books, 1999).

2. Henry Bromell, *Little America* (New York: Knopf, 2001), reviewed in James Buchan, "The Spook," *New York Times,* June 17, 2001.

3. Robert Baer, *See No Evil* (London: Arrow Books, 2002).

2. First Reactions

1. Ann Zwicker Kerr, *Come with Me from Lebanon: An American Family Odyssey* (Syracuse: Syracuse Univ. Press, 1994).

2. Stanley E. Kerr, *The Lions of Marash: Personal Experiences with American Near East Relief, 1919–1922* (Albany: State Univ. of New York Press, 1973).

3. Roy Mottahedeh, *The Mantle of the Prophet: Religion and Politics in Iran* (Oxford: Oneworld Publications, 1985).

3. The Antiterrorism and Effective Death Penalty Act of 1996

1. The essence of the Antiterrorism and Effective Death Penalty Act of 1996 is contained in the following extract: "A foreign state shall not be immune from the jurisdiction of courts of the United States in any case . . . in which money damages are sought against a foreign state for personal injury or death that was caused by an act of torture, extrajudicial killing, aircraft sabotage, hostage taking, or the provision of material support or resources . . . for such an act if such act or provision of material support is engaged in by an official, employee, or agent of such foreign state while acting within the scope of his or her office, employment, or agency, except that the court shall decline to hear a claim . . . if the foreign state was not designated as a state sponsor of terrorism . . . at the time the act occurred" (28 U.S.C. § 1605 [a] [7]).

2. *Daliberti v. Republic of Iraq,* 146 F. Supp. 2d 19 (D.D.C. 2001).

3. "Iran Air Flight 655," www.thefreedictionary.com.

4. Ibid.

5. Malcolm H. Kerr and El Sayed Yassin, eds., *Rich and Poor States in the Middle East: Egypt and the New Social Order* (Boulder: Westview Press, 1982), 469.

6. *Flatow v. Islamic Republic of Iran,* 999 F. Supp. 1 (D.D.C. 1998), transcript of evidenciary hearing before the Honorable Royce C. Lamberth, United States District Judge, Mar. 2, 1998, 70.

7. Giandomenico Picco, *Man Without a Gun: One Diplomat's Secret Struggle to Free the Hostages, Fight Terrorism, and End a War* (New York: Random House, 1999).

8. *Cicippio v. Islamic Republic of Iran,* 18 F. Supp. 2d 62 (D.D.C. 1998).

9. Terry Anderson, *Den of Lions: Memoirs of Seven Years* (New York: Crown, 1993).

10. *Anderson v. Islamic Republic of Iran,* 90 F. Supp. 2d 107 (D.D.C. 2000).

11. *Weir v. Islamic Republic of Iran,* Civil Action No. 1-1303-TPJ (D.D.C. 2003).

12. *Dodge v. Islamic Republic of Iran,* No. 03-252, slip op. (D.D.C. Aug. 25, 2004).

13. Brian Keenan, *An Evil Cradling* (London: Hutchinson, 1992).

14. Anderson, *Den of Lions,* 54n. 1.

15. Ibid., 54n. 2.

16. *Surette v. The Islamic Republic of Iran,* 231 F. Supp. 2d 260 (D.D.C. 2002), Opinion, 6.

17. William J. Clinton, *Public Papers of the Presidents of the United States,* "Remarks on Signing the Antiterrorism and Effective Death Penalty Act of 1996," Apr. 26, 1996. 32 Weekly Comp. Pres. Doc. 717.

4. The Decision to Take Legal Action

1. *Surette,* Opinion, 20.

2. "Belgium, Denmark, Finland, France and Sweden offer an additional compensation [beyond pain and suffering] for moral damages or for the violation of the personal integrity. . . . In the Netherlands, the compensation awarded for immaterial damages [contains] elements of both pain and suffering and moral damages, while Luxembourg [considers] pain and suffering as a kind of moral damage" (Commission of the European Communities, *Green Paper: Compensation to Crime Victims,* Brussels, Sept. 28, 2001).

3. Priscilla B. Hayner, *Unspeakable Truths* (London: Routledge, 2002), 180.

4. Hayner, *Unspeakable Truths,* 330.

5. www.sutherlandfamilyfoundation.org.

6. www.jencofoundation.org.

7. "Concern Growing as Families Bypass 9/11 Victims' Fund," *New York Times,* Aug. 31, 2003.

8. *Surette,* Opinion, 23–24.

9. *Roeder v. Islamic Republic of Iran,* 333 F.3d 228 (D.C.C. 2003).

10. *Regier v. Islamic Republic of Iran,* 281 F. Supp. 2d 87 (D.D.C. 2003); *Dammarell v. Islamic Republic of Iran,* 281 F. Supp. 2d 105, 112 (D.D.C. 2003).

11. *Kilburn v. Islamic Republic of Iran*, 277 F. Supp. 2d 24 (D.D.C. 2003); *Kilburn v. Socialist People's Libyan Arab Jamahiriya*, 2003 U.S. Dist. LEXIS 14347 (D.D.C. Aug. 8, 2003).

12. The prospect of Qaddafi's payment of compensation to American victims of the Lockerbie bombing was met with criticism in some quarters of the U.S. press. *Washington Post* columnist Jim Hoagland condemned the acceptance of Qaddafi's compensation payments in an article entitled as "Give the Devil His Due" (Aug. 10, 2003).

13. Directorate of Operations, undated, "Buckley Kidnapping Talking Points." DO 0122. DECL OADR DRV, HUM 4-82, NORTH, ALL PORTIONS SECRET. 11. Approved for Release Aug. 1997.

14. Graham Watson, *Report on the Role of the European Union in Combating Terrorism*, (2001/2016 [INI]), Committee on Citizens' Freedoms and Rights, Justice and Home Affairs, European Parliament, July 12, 2001, Explanatory Statement.

15. Commission of the European Communities, *Green Paper*.

16. Michael Martinez, "Comments Concerning Proposed European Union Legislation for Victims of Terrorism," Crowell and Moring, Washington, D.C., unpublished document, Oct. 2001.

17. Watson, *Report on the Role of the European Union*, Explanatory Statement, I. 2.

18. Hayner, *Unspeakable Truths*, 93.

19. Ibid., 102.

20. Ibid., 261–62.

21. Imperfections in the law are discussed in Michael Martinez and Stuart Newberger, "Combating State-Sponsored Terrorism with Civil Lawsuits: Anderson v. Islamic Republic of Iran and Other Cases," *Victim Advocate: The Journal of the National Crime Victim Bar Association* 3, no. 4 (Spring/Summer 2002).

22. Rama Mani, *Beyond Retribution: Seeking Justice in the Shadows of War* (Cambridge: Polity Press, 2002).

5. Knock, and the Door Shall Be Opened

1. Rashmee Z. Ahmed, "Who Did It? Osama or Mughniyeh?" *Times of India*, Sept. 19, 2001.

2. CIA Directorate of Operations, Apr. 4, 1984, 0845 hours, "Islamic Jihad Claims Responsibility for Buckley Kidnapping." DO 0122. DECL OADR DRV, HUM 4-82, NORTH, ALL PORTIONS SECRET. 7. Approved for release Aug. 1997.

3. CIA Directorate of Operations, undated, "Buckley Kidnapping Talking Points."

4. Ibid.

5. CIA Directorate of Operations, June 25, 1984, "Buckley Kidnapping Update." DO 1846. DECL OADR DRV, HUM 4-82, NORTH, ALL PORTIONS SECRET. 12. Approved for release Aug. 1997.

6. *Kerr v. Islamic Republic of Iran*, testimony of Robert Oakley, 21.

7. Ibid., and *Kerr v. Islamic Republic of Iran,* testimony of Reginald Bartholomew, 41.

8. White House Office, Referral, 8615453, May 19, 1986. Unclassified by United States Department of State Review Authority, Nov. 8, 2002 (ID 2002 200101937).

9. Anderson, *Den of Lions,* 54.

10. Juan R. I. Cole and Nikki R. Keddie, eds., *Shi'ism and Social Protest* (New Haven: Yale Univ. Press, 1986), dedication and preface.

11. Kerr and Yassin, *Rich and Poor States,* 469.

12. Magnus Ranstorp, *Hizb'allah in Lebanon* (London: Macmillan, 1997), 88.

13. *Kerr v. Islamic Republic of Iran,* testimony of David S. Dodge, 13.

14. Thomas Friedman, *From Beirut to Jerusalem* (New York: Doubleday, 1989), 180.

15. Baer, *See No Evil.*

16. Carol Marsh, *United We Stand: America's War Against Terrorism. Factual, Tactful Information to Help Us All Help All Kids!* (Peachtree City: Gallopade International, 2001).

17. Ranstorp, *Hizb'allah in Lebanon,* 34.

18. Ibid., 35.

19. Ibid., 31.

20. Ibid., 79–80.

21. Ibid., 68.

22. Ibid., 62.

23. Ibid., 31.

24. Ibid., 62.

25. Ibid., 63.

26. Ibid., 90.

27. Ibid., 88.

28. Ibid., 91.

29. *Kerr v. Islamic Republic of Iran,* testimony of David S. Dodge, 15.

30. Ibid.

31. Ranstorp, *Hizb'allah in Lebanon,* 89.

32. Ibid., 91.

33. Ibid.

34. These included Jeremy Levin, Charles Glass, and Frank Regier.

35. U.S. Department of State, Information Memorandum, Feb. 10, 1984, Jonathan T. How to The Secretary, T4 FES II A9 .11, Clearance JCS/J-3: Col Dsallee.

6. Words Remembered

1. S. Seikaly, R. Baalbaki, and P. Dodd, eds., *Quest for Understanding: Arabic and Islamic Studies in Memory of Malcolm H. Kerr* (Beirut: American Univ. of Beirut, 1991), xx.

2. Malcolm Kerr, *The Arab Cold War* (London: Oxford Univ. Press, 1971), v.

3. Kerr and Yassin, *Rich and Poor States,* 450.

4. Ibrahim Abu-Lughod, ed., *The Arab-Israeli Confrontation of June 1967: An Arab Perspective* (Evanston: Northwestern Univ. Press, 1970), vii.

5. Malcolm H. Kerr, "The West and the Middle East: The Light and the Shadow," Middle East Studies Association Bulletin 7, no. 1 (Feb. 1, 1973).

6. Malcolm H. Kerr, "Blowup in the Middle East—the Danger Remains: Israel's Threats Against Lebanon and the PLA Carry Wide Implications," *Los Angeles Times*, Mar. 12, 1982.

7. Ranstorp, *Hizb'allah in Lebanon*, 31.

8. The Mourabitoun is a secular Nasserite organization opposed to Maronite Christian political domination of Lebanon. During the Lebanese civil war, it operated its own armed militia.

9. U.S. Dept. of State, American Embassy Beirut to Secretary of State Washington D.C., Jan. 26, 1983, Subject: Dodge Kidnapping, DOC_NBR: 1983BEIRUT00954.

10. U.S. Dept. of State, Secretary of State Washington D.C. to American Embassy Beirut, May 17, 1983, Subject: Dodge Kidnapping, DOC_NBR: 1983STATE135755.

11. U.S. Dept. of State, American Embassy Beirut to Secretary of State Washington D.C., May 17, 1983, Subject: Dodge Kidnapping, DOC_NBR: 1983BEIRUT05728.

12. U.S. Dept. of State, American Embassy Beirut to Secretary of State Washington D.C., June 15, 1983, Subject: Dodge Kidnapping, DOC_NBR: 1983BEIRUT06722. Ironically, the wife of the author of the telex, Robert Pugh, who later became ambassador to Chad, was killed aboard the French airline UTA Flight 72, destroyed by a bomb en route from Brazzaville to Paris on September 19, 1989 (discussed in chap. 3). Eventually Robert Pugh would become a plaintiff in a civil suit against the Libyan government, under the terms of the Antiterrorism Act (*Pugh v. Socialist People's Libyan Arab Jamahiriya*, 290 F. Supp. 2d 54 (D.D.C. 2003).

13. U.S. Dept. of State, American Embassy Beirut to Secretary of State Washington D.C., June 23, 1983, Subject: Dodge Kidnapping, DOC_NBR: 1983BEIRUT07001.

14. "What's News—Worldwide," *Wall Street Journal*, Jan. 19, 1984; U.S. Dept. of State, Secretary of State Washington D.C. to American Embassy Moscow, Feb. 1, 1984, Subject: Middle East Mission—Meeting with Cheysson, Jan. 19, 1984, DOC_NBR: 1984STATE030612.

15. *Kerr v. Islamic Republic of Iran*, testimony of Reginald Bartholomew, 36.

16. Anderson, *Den of Lions*, 51.

17. *Kerr*, testimony of Reginald Bartholomew, 33.

18. Directorate General of Internal Security Forces, Command: Beirut Police, Brigade: Beirut Regional, Squad: Hubeish, Police Station: Hubeish, No.: 85/02, Subject: Investigating the assassination of the President of the American University of Beirut Malcolm Kerr, Jan. 24, 1984. (English translation: a true copy pursuant to the instructions of the General Prosecutor in Beirut No. 22420—Feb. 6, 2003).

19. National Security Council, Memorandum for Anne Higgins from Robert M. Kimmitt, Subject: Note of Sympathy to Mrs. Kerr, Jan. 30, 1984, 0793, with attachments.

20. U.S. Dept. of State, Information Memorandum, Feb. 10, 1984, Jonathan T. How to The Secretary.

Epilogue

1. *Foremost-McKesson, Inc. v. Islamic Republic of Iran,* 905 F.2d 438 (D.C.Cir. 1990).

2. Robert Fisk, "He Takes His Secrets to the Grave," *Independent,* Dec. 31, 2006.

3. Claudia Roden, *A Book of Middle Eastern Food* (New York: Knopf, 1968).

4. Kim Ghattas, "Lebanon's Groundbreaking Tribunal," *BBC News,* news.bbc.co.uk, Apr. 21, 2006.

Bibliography

Abu-Lughod, Ibrahim, ed. *The Arab-Israeli Confrontation of June 1967: An Arab-Perspective.* Evanston: Northwestern Univ. Press, 1970.

Ahmed, Rashmee Z. "Who Did It? Osama or Mughniyeh?" *Times of India.* Sept. 19, 2001.

Alejandre v. Republic of Cuba. 996 F. Supp. 1239 (S.D. Fla. 1997).

Anderson, Terry. *Den of Lions: Memoirs of Seven Years.* New York: Crown, 1993.

Anderson v. Islamic Republic of Iran. 90 F. Supp. 2d 107 (D.D.C. 2000).

Antiterrorism and Effective Death Penalty Act of 1996. 28 U.S.C. § 1605 (a) (7).

Baer, Robert. *See No Evil: The True Story of a Ground Soldier in the CIA's War on Terrorism.* London: Arrow Books, 2002.

Blundy, Anna. *Every Time We Say Goodbye: The Story of a Father and a Daughter.* London: Arrow Books, 1999.

Bromell, Henry. *Little America.* New York: Knopf, 2001.

CIA Directorate of Operations. "Islamic Jihad Claims Responsibility for Buckley Kidnapping." Apr. 4, 1984, 0845 hours. DO 0122. DECL OADR DRV, HUM 4-82, NORTH, ALL PORTIONS SECRET. 7. Approved for release Aug. 1997.

———. "Buckley Kidnapping Talking Points." Undated. DO 0122. DECL OADR DRV, HUM 4-82, NORTH, ALL PORTIONS SECRET. 11. Approved for release Aug. 1997.

———. "Buckley Kidnapping Update." June 25, 1984. DO 1846. DECL OADR DRV, HUM 4-82, NORTH, ALL PORTIONS SECRET. 12. Approved for release Aug. 1997.

Cicippio v. Islamic Republic of Iran. 18 F. Supp. 2d 62 (D.D.C. 1998).

Clinton, William J. "Remarks on Signing the Antiterrorism and Effective Death Penalty Act of 1996." Apr. 26, 1996. 32 *Weekly Compilation of Presidential Documents.* 717.

Cole, Juan R. I., and Nikki R. Keddie, eds. *Shi'ism and Social Protest.* New Haven: Yale Univ. Press, 1986.

Commission of the European Communities. *Green Paper: Compensation to Crime Victims.* Brussels, Sept. 28, 2001.

"Concern Growing as Families Bypass 9/11 Victims' Fund." *New York Times,* Aug. 31, 2003.

Daliberti v. Republic of Iraq. 146 F. Supp. 2d 19 (D.D.C. 2001).

Dammarell v. Islamic Republic of Iran. 281 F. Supp. 2d 105, 112 (D.D.C. 2003).

Directorate General of Internal Security Forces, Command: Beirut Police, Brigade: Beirut Regional, Squad: Hubeish, Police Station: Hubeish, No.: 85/02. Subject: Investigating the assassination of the President of the American University of Beirut Malcolm Kerr. Jan. 24, 1984.

Dodge v. Islamic Republic of Iran. No. 03-252, slip op. (D.D.C. Aug. 25, 2004).

Fisk, Robert. "He Takes His Secrets to the Grave." *The Independent,* Dec. 31, 2006.

———. *Pity the Nation: Lebanon at War.* Oxford: Oxford Univ. Press, 1990.

Flatow v. Islamic Republic of Iran. 999 F. Supp. 1 (D.D.C. 1998).

Foremost-McKesson, Inc. v. Islamic Republic of Iran. 905 F.2d 438 (D.C.Cir. 1990).

Friedman, Thomas. *From Beirut to Jerusalem.* New York: Doubleday, 1989.

Ghattas, Kim. "Lebanon's Groundbreaking Tribunal." *BBC News,* news.bbc.co.uk, Apr. 21, 2006.

Hayner, Priscilla B. *Unspeakable Truths: Facing the Challenge of Truth Commissions.* London: Routledge, 2002.

Hoagland, Jim. "Give the Devil His Due." *Washington Post,* Aug. 10, 2003.

Hourani, Albert. *A History of the Arab Peoples.* London: Faber and Faber, 1991.

Huntington, Samuel P. *The Clash of Civilizations and the Remaking of World Order.* London: Free Press, 2002.

Ibrahim, Saad Eddin. *The New Arab Social Order: A Study of the Social Impact of Oil Wealth.* Boulder: Westview Press, 1982.

Jenco v. Islamic Republic of Iran. 154 F. Supp. 2d 27 (D.D.C. 2001).

Justice for Victims of Terrorism Act, Public Law 106-386, 114 Stat. 1464 2000, section 2002.

Keenan, Brian. *An Evil Cradling.* London: Hutchinson, 1992.

Kerr, Ann Zwicker. *Come with Me from Lebanon: An American Family Odyssey.* Syracuse: Syracuse Univ. Press, 1994.

Kerr, Malcolm H. *The Arab Cold War.* London: Oxford Univ. Press, 1971.

————. "Blowup in the Middle East—the Danger Remains: Israel's Threats Against Lebanon and the PLA Carry Wide Implications" *Los Angeles Times,* Mar. 12, 1983.

————. *Islamic Reform: The Political and Legal Theories of Muhammad 'Abduh and Rashid Rida.* Berkeley and Los Angeles: Univ. of California Press, 1966.

————. "The West and the Middle East: The Light and the Shadow," *Middle East Studies Association Bulletin 7,* no. 1 (Feb. 1973): 1–8.

Kerr, Malcolm H., and El Sayed Yassin, eds. *Rich and Poor States in the Middle East: Egypt and the New Social Order.* Boulder: Westview Press, 1982.

Kerr, Stanley E. *The Lions of Marash: Personal Experiences with American Near East Relief, 1919–1922.* Albany: State Univ. of New York Press, 1973.

Kerr v. Islamic Republic of Iran. 245 F. Supp. 2d 59 (D.D.C. 2003).

Kilburn v. Islamic Republic of Iran. 277 F. Supp. 2d 24 (D.D.C. 2003).

Kilburn v. Socialist People's Libyan Arab Jamahiriya. 2003 U.S. Dist. LEXIS 14347 (D.D.C. Aug. 8, 2003).

Levin, Sis. *Beirut Diary: A Husband Held Hostage and a Wife Determined to Set Him Free.* Downers Grove, Ill.: Intervarsity Press, 1989.

Mani, Rama. *Beyond Retribution: Seeking Justice in the Shadows of War.* Cambridge: Polity Press, 2002.

Marsh, Carol. *United We Stand: America's War Against Terrorism. Factual, Tactful Information to Help Us All Help All Kids!* Peachtree City: Gallopade International, 2001.

Martinez, Michael. "Comments Concerning Proposed European Union Legislation for Victims of Terrorism." Crowell and Moring, Washington, D.C., unpublished document, Oct. 2001.

Martinez, Michael, and Stuart Newberger. "Combating State-Sponsored Terrorism With Civil Lawsuits: Anderson v. Islamic Republic of Iran and Other Cases." *Victim Advocate: The Journal of the National Crime Victim Bar Association* 3, no. 4 (Spring/Summer 2002).

Mottahedeh, Roy. *The Mantle of the Prophet: Religion and Politics in Iran.* Oxford: Oneworld Publications, 1985.

National Security Council. Memorandum for Anne Higgins from Robert M. Kimmitt, Subject: Note of Sympathy to Mrs. Kerr, Jan. 30, 1984, 0793, with attachments.

Norton, Augustus Richard. *Hizballah of Lebanon: Extremist Ideals vs. Mundane Politics.* New York: Council of Foreign Relations, 1999.

Picco, Giandomenico. *Man Without a Gun: One Diplomat's Secret Struggle to Free the Hostages, Fight Terrorism, and End a War.* New York: Random House, 1999.

Pugh v. Socialist People's Libyan Arab Jamahiriya. 290 F. Supp.2d 54 (D.D.C. 2003).

Ranstorp, Magnus. *Hizb'allah in Lebanon: The Politics of the Western Hostage Crisis.* London: Macmillan, 1997.

Regier v. Islamic Republic of Iran. 281 F. Supp. 2d 87 (D.D.C. 2003).

Roden, Claudia. *A Book of Middle Eastern Food.* New York: Knopf, 1968.

Roeder v. Islamic Republic of Iran. 333 F.3d 228 (D.C.C. 2003).

Rushdie, Salman. *The Satanic Verses.* London: Viking, 1988.

Seikaly, S., R. Baalbaki, and P. Dodd, eds. *Quest for Understanding: Arabic and Islamic Studies in Memory of Malcolm H. Kerr.* Beirut: American Univ. of Beirut, 1991.

Surette v. The Islamic Republic of Iran. 231 F. Supp.2d 260 (D.D.C. 2002).

Sutherland v. Republic of Iran. 151 F. Supp. 2d 27 (D.D.C. 2001).

U.S. Department of State. American Embassy Beirut to Secretary of State Washington D.C., Jan. 26, 1983, Subject: Dodge Kidnapping, DOC_NBR: 1983BEIRUT00954.

———. American Embassy Beirut to Secretary of State Washington D.C., May 17, 1983, Subject: Dodge Kidnapping, DOC_NBR: 1983BEIRUT05728.

———. American Embassy Beirut to Secretary of State Washington D.C., June 15, 1983, Subject: Dodge Kidnapping, DOC_NBR: 1983BEIRUT06722.

———. American Embassy Beirut to Secretary of State Washington D.C., June 23, 1983, Subject: Dodge Kidnapping, DOC_NBR: 1983BEIRUT07001.

———. Information Memorandum, Feb. 10, 1984, Jonathan T. How to The Secretary, T4 FES II A9 .11, Clearance JCS/J-3: Col Dsallee.

———. Secretary of State Washington D.C. to American Embassy Beirut, May 17, 1983, Subject: Dodge Kidnapping, DOC_NBR: 1983STATE135755.

———. Secretary of State Washington D.C. to American Embassy Moscow, Feb. 1, 1984, Subject: Middle East Mission—Meeting with Cheysson, Jan. 19, 1984, DOC_NBR: 1984STATE030612.

Watson, Graham. *Report on the Role of the European Union in Combating Terrorism.* (2001/2016 [INI]), Committee on Citizens' Freedoms and Rights, Justice and Home Affairs, European Parliament, July 12, 2001.

Weir v. Islamic Republic of Iran. Civil Action No. 1-1303-TPJ (D.D.C. 2003).

White House Office, Referral, 8615453, May 19, 1986. Unclassified by United States Department of State Review Authority, Nov. 8, 2002 (ID 2002 200101937).

Index

Certain main headings are abbreviated in the subentries: AUB (American University of Beirut), AUC (American University in Cairo), Antiterrorism Act (Antiterrorism and Effective Death Penalty Act), AZK (Ann Kerr), MHK (Malcolm Kerr), *Kerr v. Iran (Kerr v. Islamic Republic of Iran)*, Letters (Kerr, Malcolm [LETTERS]), UCLA (University of California at Los Angeles). Page numbers in italic denote illustrations or maps.

Other titles in Contemporary Issues in the Middle East

Citizenship and the State in the Middle East: Approaches and Applications
    Nils A. Butenschon, Uri Davis, and Manuel Hassassian, eds.

Come with Me from Lebanon: An American Family Odyssey
    Ann Zwicker Kerr

The Druze and Their Faith in Tawhid
    Anis Obeid

Gender and Citizenship in the Middle East
    Suad Joseph, ed.

Islam Without Illusions: Its Past, Its Present, and Its Challenges for the Future
    Ed Hotaling

The Kurdish National Movement: Its Origins and Development
    Wadie Jwaideh

Painting the Middle East
    Ann Zwicker Kerr

Turkish Islam and the Secular State: The Gülen Movement
    M. Hakan Yavuz and John L. Esposito, eds.

Twenty Years of Islamic Revolution: Political and Social Transition in Iran since 1979
    Eric Hooglund, ed.

Writing Off the Beaten Track: Reflections on the Meaning of Travel and Culture in the Middle East
    Judith Caesar